Operation Timothy *Signature* LG

Leader's GUIDE

CHRISTIAN BUSINESS MENS CONNECTION

Operation Timothy ©2008 by CBMC, Inc.
Operation Timothy Signature, Second edition, Book 2 ©2011 by CBMC, Inc.

All rights reserved, including translation.

All Scripture quotations, unless otherwise indicated, are taken from the Holy Bible,
New International Version®, NIV®. Copyright ©1973, 1978, 1984, 2011 by Biblica, Inc.™

Used by permission of Zondervan. All rights reserved worldwide. www.zondervan.com
The "NIV" and "New International Version" are trademarks registered in the United States
Patent and Trademark Office by Biblica, Inc.™

Printed and Bound in the United States of America
ISBN 1-947457-03-9
ISBN 978-1-947457-03-4

CBMC is Christian Business mens Connection.

Table of Contents

Leader's GUIDE

i.	Principles of Effective Discipleship	BK1: 4
ii.	Life Questions	
	1. What Is the Purpose of Life?	BK1: 16
	2. Is the Bible Credible?	BK1: 19
	3. Where Is God?	BK1: 24
	4. Who Is Jesus?	BK1: 28
	5. Why Did Jesus Come?	BK1: 31
	6. Can I Be Accepted and Forgiven?	BK1: 36
iii.	Life Foundations	
	1. New Life in Christ	BK2: 1
	2. Our New Identity	BK2: 6
	3. Battling with the World, the Flesh, & the Devil	BK2: 10
	4. Dealing with Temptation	BK2: 14
	5. Discovering the Holy Spirit	BK2: 18
	6. Communicating with God	BK2: 23
	7. Telling Others Our Story	BK2: 27
iv.	Life Perspectives	
	1. Digging into the Bible	BK3: 1
	2. Knowing God's Will	BK3: 6
	3. Becoming a Person of Character	BK3: 10
	4. Relationships	BK3: 14
	5. Kingdom Perspectives	BK3: 17
	6. Your Calling as an Insider	BK3: 23
	7. Multiplying Your Life	BK3: 27
v.	Conclusions and Recommendations	BK3: 32
vi.	Index of Operation Timothy Books	BK3: 39

Operation Timothy
Leader's Guide

Operation Timothy is an investigative Bible study with the goal of helping people to grow spiritually. This Leader's guide is designed for use by a facilitator in a one-on-one or small group situation as a link with the *Living Proof Evangelism and Discipleship* series.

How To Use This Guide

Operation Timothy (OT) is designed to be used in a one-on-one situation or small group setting. It may be used with new Christians or with those who are investigating the claims of Christ. Originally designed for application in men's groups, the material has been rewritten to exclude gender specific language so as not to limit its use with women.

This leader's guide follows the format of the three OT books. It has been written to keep preparation time to a minimum in order to provide additional time for you as the leader to pray for and interact with your Timothy. Our approach is not content vs. relationship; rather we encourage a balance of both. The leader's guide is arranged to give you a visual picture of where you are. On each page you will find images corresponding with study book and notes with helpful teaching tips.

In an effort to continually improve our materials, we encourage your suggestions and observations. Our goal is to serve the Christian community at-large, as well as members of CBMC in the United States and abroad by providing high quality, cost effective materials to reach and disciple men and women for Christ.

Operation Timothy: The Purpose

You are embarking on something big: the awesome privilege of being involved in the plans of God. People are at the heart of God. He desires an increasingly intimate relationship with us. God has specifically chosen us to be His light and extend His love to His world. It is not an option.

God has an intense desire for people to be rightly related to Him: "He desires all men to be saved and come to the knowledge of Him" (1 Timothy 2:4). God did not choose angels or His creation to articulate this good news of Jesus Christ, and He did not choose a few gifted individuals to be His messengers. He chose every believer to be a witness of His glory in their words, in their conduct, in their attitudes— in summation, their very lives (Matthew 5:16).

Yet just as babies need to grow and be taught how to communicate, so it is with new believers. This growth and teaching of new believers is at the heart of discipleship. Discipleship is God's means of maturing a new Christian to accomplish the following: for each individual to grow in an intimate relationship with his Lord, to be a life witness of Christ to a searching world, to offer love and care to the hurting and desperate, and to be interdependent in meeting each others' needs.

Operation Timothy is not just a curriculum or program that teaches information and principles. It is an opportunity for you to enter into a relationship with another believer or seeker, either one-on-one or with several in a small group. The purpose is that each person will grow in intimacy with God and catch the vision of multiplying disciples. God uses every person who is indwelt by Christ to reach the next generation. With each new generation following our Lord Christ Jesus, our Father's glory is extended to the end of the earth and to the end of time. So the process of OT is something larger than you, and yet it allows you to leverage your impact in this world.

Multiplied thousands have entered into the OT process and have been dramatically changed. Don't hesitate to enter as a disciple or as a discipler. God will touch you, mold you and use you for His kingdom purpose. In Isaiah 60:22, God promises the people of Israel to make the least and the smallest of them a mighty nation. He is looking for people who will love, follow and obey Him. It is this promise and moreover this vision that has fired many people to enter into the life-changing process of *Operation Timothy*, that **"one shall become a thousand"** (KJV). Fruitfulness is the result of a life yielded to God to be used by Him.

CBMC and the Relational Approach

More than eighty years ago, leaders of Christian Business Mens Connection (CBMC) recognized a problem. Americans needed Christ, but many men would never hear the gospel, because they never went to church. They spent most of their time in business. CBMC leaders sought to take the good news into the business community and thereby change the country and perhaps the entire world.

In CBMC, we take the battle for souls into the world's marketplace and neighborhoods. Rather than using formulas or classes, we present the gospel through relationships. To that end, this leader's guide will often suggest questions to consider that relate content to context and learning to life. This will help keep you both from merely intellectualizing your experience. This is practical stuff. You will study and discuss such topics as faith in the home, the handling of money and living your faith at work.

The Goal of the Process

Keep the "big picture" in mind during each session. What is the bottom line? What's the central purpose of the lesson? As you approach each lesson, look for opportunities to connect with Christ. How often do we perform a full slate of Christian activities without sharing the company of the One

> TELL ME AND I FORGET;
> SHOW ME AND I REMEMBER;
> INVOLVE ME AND I UNDERSTAND.
>
> SIOUX INDIAN PROVERB

who is at the center of them? For the process to be effective, it must begin with you. You must be connected to Christ. Be sure you are in the Word of God on a daily basis. The fact is you cannot teach the reality of Christ if He is not a reality to you. Timothy needs to see Jesus living in and through another human. It will give him the desire to experience what he sees being lived out before him.

The Principles of Effective Discipleship

1. The Principle of the Spiritual Growth Process

As believers, we are called to make disciples (Matt. 28:19-20). If we examine Christ's command in Matthew 28, we see that evangelism and discipleship are one process. The Bible uses the metaphors of farming and parenting to describe it. When the Scriptures speak of evangelism, almost without exception, it uses the picture of a farmer tilling the soil, planting seed and harvesting the produce.

Parenting begins after harvesting. For example, the apostle Paul writes, "My dear children, for whom I am again in the pains of childbirth until Christ has formed you" (Galatians 4:19). To the church in Thessalonica he writes, "But we were gentle among you, like a mother caring for her children…for you know that we dealt with each of you as a Father deals with his own children…" (1 Thessalonians 2:7,11). Peter spoke of "newborn babies." John repeatedly addressed his readers as "dear children." The author of Hebrews talks about spiritual infancy and the importance of moving to adulthood. As farmers, we cultivate relationships with non-believers, allowing them to witness firsthand the power of a changed life.

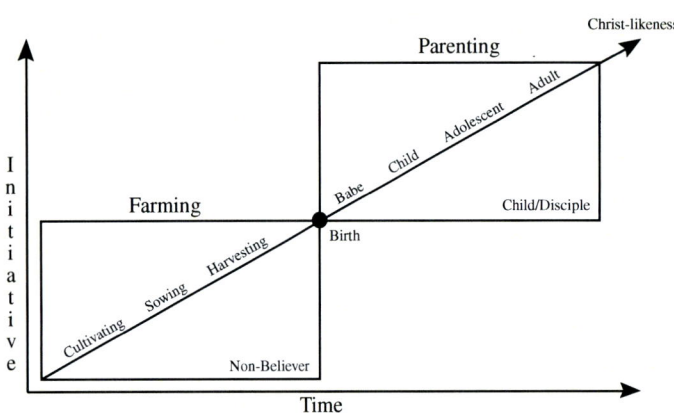

Once a person becomes a believer, our role changes to that of spiritual parent. Just as with any newborn, spiritual babes are fragile and require a lot of time and energy. But as we continue the life-on-life process, modeling the way and helping the young believer grow into adulthood, our initiative decreases as we allow him to flourish and eventually reproduce. This is not a program. It's a long process.

2. The Principle of Spiritual Farming

Spiritual farming consists of three phases: cultivating, sowing and harvesting.

CULTIVATING – Before we can sow seed, we must break up the hard ground, removing rocks, roots and other debris. If the soil is the human heart, God must remove obstacles and prepare it to receive the Word. Cultivation begins with a relationship, and relationships work through common ground. Activities, sports, computers, cooking, music — all can become the common ground of a new relationship. In 1 Corinthians 9:19-23, Paul tells how he related to different kinds of people in order to lead them to Christ. He met people at their point of need. Jesus did too. He went to them. In doing so, He was known as a friend of sinners. He didn't think that was such a bad thing. Our call is to do the same.

SOWING – The goal of sowing is to bring the unbeliever to a place where they ask the question, "Who is Jesus?" It may take years. Along the way, believers must be patient and consistent. But when the unbelieving friend is comfortable enough with us, and they like what they see, we can sow the Word.

Remember, we are to be "salt and light" (Matthew 5:13-14). Salt causes thirst. Light illuminates. *Operation Timothy* is designed to sow the Word.

HARVESTING – We can cultivate and sow for years and never see a harvest. We must leave that to God. Paul tells us in 1 Corinthians 3:6-7 that, "I planted, Apollos watered, but God was causing the growth. So then, neither the one who plants nor the one who waters is anything, but God who causes the growth." This is a long process. It takes time to turn hard, rocky clay into fertile, crop-producing soil. As we walk in obedience, we still share in the joy of that person coming into the kingdom of God. When we see a person come to know Christ, the metaphor shifts from that of farmer to that of parent.

3. The Principle of Spiritual Parenting (Life on Life)

Most people in western culture approach the subject of discipleship in a systematic, logical manner. We create an agenda, formulate a plan, and launch out — often oblivious to the needs of the person with whom we are attempting to share our life in Christ. The approach of Jesus followed the patterns indigenous to ancient Palestine. As a Rabbi (teacher), Jesus spent time with his followers. His disciples had the opportunity to observe his reactions to the rich, the poor, the priests, and the politicians. He was constantly asking questions, forcing them to think through choices and weigh events against the teachings of Scripture.

Jesus was very practical, too. He discussed the purpose and use of money, the importance of family, and the role of government. For over three years, His disciples were engaged in a life-on-life course on how to live for God in a fallen world.

For the Duration

Life-on-life discipleship is a long-term commitment. This kind of relationship requires sacrifice and may seem too costly to some. Those who see the end from the beginning possess the vision necessary for success. In His work with the twelve, Jesus did not see His ministry in their lives as something that could be put on the calendar or measured in terms of hours, days or weeks. In the three years He spent with His disciples, Jesus was absolutely devoted to them. His commitment was unlimited.

It is interesting to note that Jesus took into account changing roles and situations. For example, He dealt with Peter in a different manner than He did with Bartholomew. As a spiritual parent, you will be wise to keep in mind the stages of spiritual growth in Timothy. Infants, children, and adolescent children of God require flexibility with schedules and materials. If you have children of your own, you will see the parallels. As you deal with Timothy, begin with the patience required of a parent with a newborn and adjust your expectations as growth occurs.

Jim Peterson states:

"Our tendency is to create programs for discipleship and offer them to people as a substitute for parental care. We put people through a prescribed curriculum and expect that to take care of their needs. It doesn't work. It doesn't work because their primary need at this stage is not for information. Caring relationships are far more important to the early stages.

"New Christians need a meaningful relationship with spiritual parents. It's a primary spiritual need, along with their need for Scripture. If study guides are used, they need to be carefully chosen. They must guide people into Scripture, and the content of those guides must truly correspond with needs. If we fail to connect these matters of relationships and appropriate content, the new Christian will often just stall out in his or her growth. They might do the studies and show up with all the right answers, but still flunk the test in true spiritual growth."

Care must be taken not to extend this idea of spiritual parenthood to the point where one person virtually takes over the life of another. This kind of control becomes bizarre and creates dependency. Paul said, "Not that we lord it over your faith, but we work with you for your joy, because it is by faith you stand firm."

4. The Principle of Reproduction and Multiplication (The New Math)

In the first pages of the Bible, we discover one of the purposes of man on earth: reproduction and multiplication. The same is true in the spiritual dimension.

A Spiritual Baby Boom

In the New Testament, we see roots of the spiritual family tree to which all believers are connected. Jesus began with twelve, teaching and living the principles of a life lived under God's authority. We are the spiritual descendants of those twelve men.

Of course, the principle of exponential growth does not require the number twelve. For example, if you as an individual were to reach and cultivate two new believers over a two-year period, and continued this practice (and they did likewise) for 25 years, you would produce over a thousand spiritual descendants.

Isaiah 60:22 says, "The least of you will become a thousand, the smallest a mighty nation." And remember, while some might not be faithful, others will reach more than two — and many will have families that number in the tens of thousands. It is a formula for changing the world.

Fruitful Labors

In John 15:16, Jesus tells His followers to, "Go and bear fruit." A fully loaded apple tree is the result of one small seed. Who knows where those seeds will scatter and take root? How many new trees will grow as a result of that first, small, seemingly insignificant seed? We will never see the fruits of our labors in our lifetime. Yes, we will enjoy the fellowship and companionship of the first seeds, and first fruit, but long after we are gone, countless others will follow.

Just as parents enjoy the rich rewards and the unique experience that comes with raising children, we as spiritual parents do the same. In the end, we find ourselves closer to God, more in line with what He desires during our stay on earth.

5. The Principle of Being an Insider

The decision to follow Christ carries radical, possibly even traumatic, implications. It is a watershed in one's life. When the difference between the church and the world is so extreme, the tendency is for the Christian to bail out of society completely, seeking refuge in cloistered fellowship. In 1 Corinthians 7, the Apostle Paul repeats three times the command for the believers to remain in the situation in which God has called them. We are instructed to stay put and make a difference where we are.

Bloom Where You're Planted

The implications are significant for Timothy. If married to an unsaved spouse, remain in the marriage. If working in the midst of a pagan culture or a spiritually hostile work environment, stay there and make a difference. This may seem to be a radical prescription for a young, fragile Christian. Again, the tendency of new and excited converts will be to immerse themselves in activities and Christian fellowship. Yet this kind of young believer, with a fresh commitment and reckless enthusiasm, often has the greatest impact for Christ. The rest of us, sadly enough, become more and more enmeshed in activities that take us deeper into fellowship with other Christians while at the same time distancing ourselves from those God has given us to reach with the good news. When Paul says to remain where we are, he means new Christians have a great opportunity to influence others in the marketplace.

As you share your life with Timothy, you may need to make some effort to encourage him not to bail out as a player. The tension will come as a result of Timothy's drive to purity while attempting to maintain the vital position for influence with old friends and associates.

A Child Shall Lead Them

How ironic that God is positioning infants to accomplish His greatest works of evangelism! These people have not been branded as fanatics. They continue to have the trust of the crowd. Your role is to counsel, encourage and listen to Timothy. Encourage Timothy to begin sharing the gospel with others now. Explain that there is no need to wait until someone has completed several discipleship courses to start telling others about Jesus Christ. His work in the Great Commission begins now. In summary, we as believers are to serve on the "inside" in our culture as active agents of change. And we do it now, not tomorrow or next week.

6. The Principle of Being a Laborer

In Matthew 9:36, we pick up a conversation Jesus is having with the twelve. The Bible says, "…He had compassion on them, because they were harassed and helpless, like sheep without a shepherd." Turning to His inner circle of disciples, the Lord continues, "…the harvest is plentiful but the workers are few. Ask the Lord of the harvest, therefore, to send out workers into his harvest field" (Matthew 9:37-38). Each individual life is compared to a crop needing to be tended, watered, prepared and ultimately reaped. Send out workers! This is God's pressing desire. With more people walking the earth than at any time in history, the harvest field is almost beyond imagination. There is an urgent need to pray that God will use us to equip, train, and send out more laborers. That is the essence of discipleship.

Go With the Flow

To become an effective discipler, we must first be a disciple. There is always the temptation to feed others while depriving ourselves. However, if we constantly give, and do not receive, we will dry up and have little to give the cause of Christ. Therefore it is of vital importance as you disciple a young Christian that you continue to seek God, stay grounded in His Word, develop your prayer life and stay close to other growing Christians.

Eight Qualities of an Effective Discipler

Some people doubt that they have the skills or time to become a discipler. Ultimately, it is a matter of obedience. Just as few of us feel ready to become biological parents, few feel ready to take on the nurture and care of a spiritual infant. The following qualities are the ingredients of an effective disciple-maker:

- LOVE OF GOD: the quality of an infectious love of God,

- LOVE OF PEOPLE: the ability to help Timothy learn to love others as God does,

- VISION: the ability to see Timothy as he can be, while accepting him where he is,

- FAITHFULNESS: the ability to depend on God to be consistent,

- DEPENDABILITY: the availability that will help Timothy trust you,

- HEART OF A TEACHER: the ability to look for a teachable moment,

- SERVANTHOOD: the quality of a humble heart, the willingness to sacrifice for Timothy's needs,

- DURABILITY: a heart that says, "Whatever it takes."

7. The Principle of Spiritual Transformation

Authentic Christian growth comes from the inside and works its way to the surface—just the opposite of the manner we so often seek to impose. When we foolishly measure a new Christian's progress based on the trappings of spirituality (the right words, the correct do's and don'ts), we settle for the good over the best, the expedient over the extraordinary.

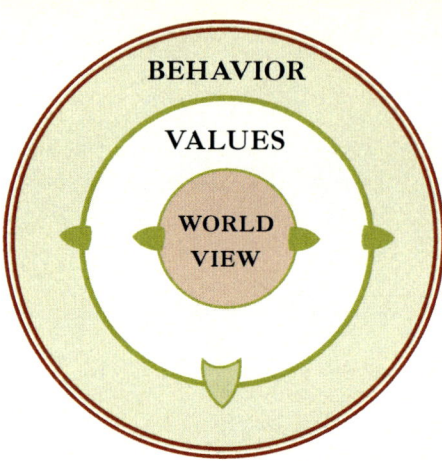

Spiritual change starts from within; it is a transformation. It is the heart motivation that must change, and that revolutionary kind of transformation takes place on three fronts: worldview, values and behavior. Discipleship focuses first on worldview: my view of God and God's view of the world. This is where I answer the big questions of life: How did I get here? Where am I going? Who is in charge? My answer to these will affect my value system: what is important to me, what I will die for, etc. My behavior, then, is a direct outgrowth of my worldview and my values. Much of spiritual growth in the past focused on behavior first. We tried to clean people up on the outside (reformation) without a change on the inside (transformation). This spiritual transformation begins with God. Philippians 1:6 says it best: "He who began a good work in me will perfect it…" It is the role of the Holy Spirit and God's Word to establish and build us spiritually. "Christ is my life" is the ultimate goal in our walk (Colossians 3:4). It is a life yielded to and drawing upon the Spirit of God within us. God's role is to grow us to maturity; our role as a spiritual parent is to guide, counsel, and care for.

8. The Principle of the Three C's: Competence, Character and Community

It is the journey that brings maturity. There are no shortcuts, no substitutes, no way earn a better position along the path. Maturity takes time, commitment, and sacrifice. Jim Petersen, in his book *Lifestyle Discipleship*, discusses three central issues around which spiritual maturity is manifest: competence, character, and community.

Competence: This refers to the basics of living and working as a Christian. How does a Christian handle this or that situation? Where are the answers to be found? How can I communicate with God? It is true that a lifetime in God's Word is not enough time to understand its depth and meaning. However, we need to be competent in our knowledge of the Scripture, "correctly handling the word of truth" (2 Timothy 2:15). Beyond that, we must be skilled in how to counsel as well as listen, to articulate the gospel and basic Christian truth, to function in a small group setting and many more.

Character: This has been defined as "who you are when no one is looking." This means that our behavior is to be pleasing to God, who is watching. Not only is God watching, so is the world. It is a lifetime pursuit, and may be the most difficult of all areas in which a Christian builds spiritual maturity. Character often develops through suffering. It is a quality that is not so much built as it is forged.

Community: The final issue is that of community. In a culture characterized by the "rugged individualist," we are duped into believing that we can do this alone — just me and God in divine fellowship. The truth is that God designed a better way. We are to do it together. He created us for fellowship. Since the beginning, God has said that it is not good for humans to be alone (Genesis 2:18). We need each other.

Spiritual maturity is always framed in the context of community. It is here that we find our gifts, exercise them and look to our brothers and sisters to supply the gifts we do not possess. It is here that we find humility, receive rebuke and correction. When we become discouraged and God seems far off, it is often through the community that God reaches out to us. Here is affirmation, encouragement and accountability. Community begins for Timothy in the context of your one-on-one relationship, but Timothy will have needs you will not be able to supply. It will also take a friend, a small group, or a church fellowship to serve the needs of a new believer. Good disciplers help find a place where roots can grow.

9. The Principle of "The Balanced Life" — The Three Devotions

Finally, we must talk about maintaining a balanced focus for our lives and ministry. God has created man with three overarching needs: a need for God, a need to be involved in a cause bigger than himself and a need for one another. For man (individually and corporately) to be at peace and be fruitful here on earth, these needs must be met and must be in balance. We are called

1. to be devoted to Christ (the first commandment: love the Lord your God with all your heart, soul, and mind—Matthew 22:37-38),
2. to be devoted to one another (the second commandment: love your neighbor as yourself—Matthew 22:39),
3. to be devoted to the gospel (the great commission: "Go therefore and make disciples…" Matthew 28:18-20).

These three devotions must be in balance; if we neglect one of them, we will not be fruitful over the long haul. If, as an individual, a team, or a church, we neglect devotion to the gospel, we will become self-focused and self-absorbed, not reaching out to others. If we misuse the concept of love for one another, we hurt each other. If we aren't devoted wholeheartedly to Christ, we miss it all and walk in the flesh.

We want to see Timothy grow in these areas as we disciple him. This balance will help Timothy grow up and give away his life, rather than holding onto it. He will truly be one who becomes a thousand (Isaiah 60:22).

Getting Started

You've heard the challenge and now four words come to mind: Where do I start?

Where do I find Timothy?

Standing on the Mount of Olives, the disciples watched their leader disappear into the clouds and felt just as overwhelmed as you may feel today. But Jesus had made things clear and concise. Here is how Jesus said to do it: "You will be my witnesses in Jerusalem" (Acts 1:8). Today Jerusalem, tomorrow the world. Jerusalem was not the hometown of any of the disciples. They were practically tourists, having followed Jesus there. He ordered them to start here and now. Urgency is, therefore, a part of the equation. In this statement, there is also an emphasis on the marketplace, where the people are: the Jerusalem of any particular era.

Steps in finding Timothy

1. Ask God to make you sensitive and attentive. Look for growing relationships between you and particular friends and acquaintances. Evaluate the chemistry you share (or lack).
2. Survey the social landscape around you. Cultivate several relationships and see where they lead. Ask different acquaintances to lunch. Enlarge your circles of friendship.

3. "Raise the Flag" from time to time, that is, mention your faith in Christ. Observe the response. Try telling a faith story ("How God helped me through the time when…"). Afterward, take some time for "gardening." Watch what breaks the surface after you've planted these seeds. It may take a few days or a few weeks, or much longer.

4. Consider both non-Christians as well as young believers. The most likely person is the one you personally lead to Christ.

5. If you feel God leading you to a specific person, spend some quality time with him/her without proposing the greater commitment of a study. Invite this person to dinner. Do something recreational together over a weekend. Build informality and levity into the relationship from the beginning (it will serve you well later).

How do I invite Timothy to do *Operation Timothy*?

Ask general questions about Timothy's background, including spiritual, emotional and physical areas of life, as you spend time together. Ask God to give you discernment to recognize when He has prepared Timothy. At that time, ask Him for courage to ask Timothy to investigate the Scriptures together. Reflect on the "Spiritual Awareness Chart" below, asking God to give you insight into where Timothy is in his spiritual journey.

Don't rush or pressure. Notice the different phases of each stage in the chart. One person may quickly move through these; it may take another person years to change from an antagonistic attitude to a mere willingness to discuss spiritual issues. As finite human beings, we cannot see into another person's heart and know for certain where they are spiritually, but God's Spirit does give discernment into Timothy's spiritual needs.

If Timothy seems open, show him the *Operation Timothy* books. Explain that he will be able to investigate personally what the Bible says about various topics. Point out a few topics from the Table of Contents in Book 1. Ask Timothy if he would like to meet regularly to discuss these issues. If Timothy agrees, set a time and place to meet and give him Book 1, *Life Questions*. Ask him to complete the lesson before your appointment. Show him the question-and-answer format and the printed Scriptures in the text.

Spiritual Awareness Chart

Sanctification	**STAGE IV** **Discipling** Maturing Process Disciple = Reproduced life of Christ Emphasis: Life-on-life relationships	+4 +3 +2 +1	Going! Mobilized to reproduce Maturing into Christ-likeness Settling into a caring community Grounding in faith
Regeneration			**New Creature**
C O N V I C T I O N	**STAGE III** **Harvesting** Picking the Crop The Grain = A Decision for Jesus Christ Emphasis: Encourage a meaningful decision of faith	-1 -2 -3 -4 -5	Repenting and believing Deciding to act Recognizing personal need Positive attitude toward Gospel Grasping implications of Gospel
	STAGE II **Sowing** Planting the Seed The Seed = Gospel Truth Emphasis: Presenting the Gospel, understanding the truth.	-6 -7 -8 -9	Aware of Gospel basics Positive attitude toward the Bible Aware of Bible's relevance Aware of difference in messenger
General Revelation	**STAGE I** **Cultivation** Preparing the Soil The Soil = Human Hearts Emphasis: Building a friendship bridge	-10 -11 -12	Positive attitude toward messenger Aware of messenger Going his own way
God's Role	*Our Role*	*Mini-Decisions* Some of the specific decisions that could be made.	

(Rejection spans -6 through -12)

Where and when?

Time and place are important considerations. Find out about Timothy's schedule. A weekly lunch appointment can work, but time will be constrained. Remember, you need 90 minutes. Breakfast might be better. Most of us are sharper in the morning. An evening over a simple dinner can be an excellent time, because Timothy will tend to be under less pressure to be somewhere else. If Timothy is single, this might be your best option.

Where should you meet? Be creative. Think about a good environment for talking and praying. The clatter of a diner can be distracting. Your office is a possibility. Come to an agreement on the best time and place for both of you, and commit to it.

Here are some other points to consider as you begin. Be sure you do some of the sharing, rather than simply asking all the questions. Be open and transparent. Balance personal sharing with discussion of the Scriptural truths in the lessons. Review the previous lesson each week. Timothy might have special needs and you may fail to finish a lesson in one week. It's okay to complete the lesson the next time.

How is the weekly meeting structured?

A typical 90 minute OT session will look something like this:

Arrival and welcome	5 minutes
Fellowship and sharing	15 minutes
Scripture memory (begins in Book 2)	10 minutes
Review of previous lessons	15 minutes
Discuss major topic	30 minutes
Assignment	5 minutes
Prayer	10 minutes

No session will be exactly the same. Be flexible, but avoid the temptation to let fellowship stretch out too long, unless Timothy is in a crisis and needs time to talk.

Fellowship and Sharing

Every session should begin with relaxed conversation allowing you and Timothy to get to know one another and build a strong relationship. This relationship provides the environment for character development and ultimately determines your success as a disciple. This is an opportunity for you to identify his needs and evaluate progress. You, the leader, control the pace and direction of the conversation by asking questions. It's an excellent way to gain insight, and to express interest in his life as well.

Discussion

The key to reaching your session objective is a good start, and the key to a good start is making sure both you and Timothy know where you're going and how you're going to get there. Explain the lesson and why it is important. Too often, without such an introduction the session wanders and ends 2 hours later with little progress having been made toward the goal. Questions play a vital role in the discussion. Study Jesus' use of questions and how He guided people toward the truth through them. A good question compels the listener to discover the truth for himself. There are four basic types of questions and their value is determined, to a large extent, by the situation.

- a. Leading Question - "Paul says in Philippians that we are always to rejoice, doesn't he?" This type of question is great for a lecture, but has little value in a discussion. Little, if any, response is required. It should be used only as a last resort.

- b. Limiting Question - "What three great truths are in this passage?" This question also has limited value in a discussion. It is clear you have an exact answer in mind and this will constrain the discovery process. This type of question should only be used when Timothy has difficulty understanding the initial question and needs further clarification.

- c. Open Question - "What are some of the truths you see in this passage?" This type of question has great value in your discussion. It allows discovery of one, two, three, or even more truths. The emphasis is on discovery, not on finding the answer.

- d. Wide-Open Question - "What else do you see in this passage?" This question is an excellent way to maintain momentum in the discussion, particularly if an important point remains undiscovered.

Your discussion should contain at least 80-90% of the "open questions." These allow you to guide the discussion in such a manner that your Timothy can discover answers himself. Begin your discussion by asking an open, application-oriented question: Why is this concept important? How does it apply to us personally? Allow him to wrestle with the answer and then move to the Scriptures dealing with that concept. Continue to ask questions, using the ones you developed during your study and preparation of this subject. If he has difficulty answering a question, rephrase it or break it down into smaller, simpler questions. It would be better to ask a limiting question than to give him the answer. Otherwise, you have no way to measure his understanding. The most effective learning technique is self-discovery, and you're the guide.

Prayer

Prayer is the time you and Timothy spend directly in the presence of God. Keep in mind the importance of that statement, and avoid falling into the "punctuational prayer" trap, using it as bookends for a meeting. Timothy is learning to talk to God through your model. You'll do most of the praying in the beginning, with Timothy picking up his share as time progresses. Be sure to use language that Timothy understands.

Administration

- a. You and Timothy should meet once a week or whatever works best with your schedules.
- b. Decide which meeting time works best for the two of you.
- c. *Operation Timothy* is not a social club. *Operation Timothy* is discipleship!
- d. Everything that is spoken must be kept confidential.
- e. You should always teach personal application: How does the Word apply to Timothy?
- f. You should be creating an atmosphere for building a relationship with Timothy.
- g. You should emphasize accountability from Timothy.
- h. Timothy should notify you if he is going to miss a meeting.
- i. You should follow up if Timothy is missing an excessive number of sessions.

Operation Timothy Diary

The purpose of the diary is to record information that will help you be more effective in prayer and ministry to your "Timothy." After each session, record any new information that will help you work with him. This diary can be downloaded at http://www.operationtimothy.com/disciplemaker.

OPERATION TIMOTHY DIARY

The purpose of this diary is to record information that will help you be more effective in prayer and ministry to your Timothy. Each week, after your session, enter any new information that will help you work with him/her. Make copies of these pages as needed.

Name   Nickname

Address

City   Zip

Home Phone   Business Phone

Birthdate   Spouse's Name

Children's Names & Ages

Present Job   How long?

Previous Work

Hobbies

Other Personal Information

Sessions Notes: Progress? Does he need help with major concepts, family issues, application of principles, prayer, Scripture memory, etc.?

BK1:17

leader's guide for book 1

LIFE QUESTIONS

SUGGESTED DISCUSSIONS AND QUESTIONS

Chapter 1: What Is the Purpose of Life?

The Big Idea: To cause Timothy to step back from the busyness and challenges of everyday life and consider the big questions.

Key Teaching Point: Only by mastering the key life question, "Why am I here," can we begin to reveal our purpose in life.

Additional Discussion Questions and Illustrations

The following questions and illustrations may be helpful to stir your thinking. For the greatest impact, use these as supplemental material to your own personal illustrations. Don't tell your Timothy the answers. In Proverbs 20:5, it says, "The purpose in a man's mind is like deep waters, but a man of understanding will draw it out." A key to your success as a facilitator will be your ability to ask open-ended questions to elicit a response from Timothy.

Questions like…

"…What does that mean to you?"

"…Can you tell me more about that?"

"…Why is that significant to you?"

"…How does this question make you feel?"

Off-the-Wall Answers

Diplomacy is critically important as you establish your relationship with Timothy. There may be times when Timothy's answers or statements cause you alarm. Perhaps the best way to handle such a situation is simply to ask another question, rather than make an attempt to refute the statement. Find common ground through the use of a personal illustration and ending the story with, "I felt the same way at one time…" Keep in mind that our goal is to create an environment in which Timothy will feel safe and open up.

Working Through the Lesson

Whether or not Timothy has completed the lesson, we suggest that you proceed through the material, question by question, beginning with the "What Do People Say" section.

Teaching Outline

I. Having It All
    Some men have everything but don't know how to live.

II. Reflection
    What is a person's purpose in life?

III. We're All Wondering
    The big question of life.

IV. Why Am I here?
    Consider: What will your life add up to?

Page 1:

Q: Do you think that everything, even something as simple as a butterfly has a purpose?

What Do People Say?

Q: Which of these quotations is most striking to you? Why?

Take time to understand, to discuss, and to ask additional questions regarding Timothy's views on his purpose for life.

Q: What are your thoughts about the statement on page 2 by Vaclav Havel regarding "the tragedy of modern man"?

Having It All

Page 4:

Q: What does a decaying farm and rusting swing set make you think of?

We're All Wondering

Page 5:

Q: How do you answer the questions, "Who am I?"; "Why am I here?"; "Where did I come from?"; "Where am I going?"

Page 6:

Why Am I Here?

Q: What do you think about Ken Boa's quote at the right side of this page, "It is much wiser to follow Kierkegaard's advice to define life backward and live it forwards – start from the destiny and define the journey in light of it."?

Temporal vs. Eternal: An Illustration

Suppose someone plans to move from Dallas to Atlanta, where he knows he will spend the remaining fifty years of his life. He carefully prepares for the two-day drive by pouring over every detail of the journey, including what clothing he will wear, what rest stops he will use, where he will refuel his car, what motel he will stay at, all meals he will eat, and where he will eat them. Nothing on the journey is left to chance, but he doesn't know what he will do when he arrives in Atlanta. The absurdity of this scenario is easy to see, and yet the bulk of people we encounter are living their lives in this way. In this analogy, the two-day trip is our earthly sojourn, and the fifty-year stay is our eternal destiny. But what is obviously ludicrous on a temporal scale seems acceptable when we speak of eternity, perhaps because our eternal destiny seems so vague and wispy to many of us (Kenneth Boa, *Conformed to His Image*, page 60).

Page 7:

★ Emphasize these questions from the book.

Q: Adding value to others – What role does this concept play in shaping your purpose in life?

Q: Which of your activities make the greatest contribution to your legacy? (What does legacy mean to you?)

Next Steps

1. Set a day and time to get together again.

2. Encourage your Timothy to consider the Additional Resources and the Optional Applications. For example:

    a. Have him listen to the CD or download the message from operationtimothy.com.

    b. Set-up a time to watch *Amazing Grace* together with your spouses.

    c. Ask him about the quotation on Page 10:

    What do you think of the quote by the psychologist James Dobson?

4. Assign Chapter 2, "Is the Bible credible?" However, be sensitive. If you did not get through Chapter 1, ask Timothy to review it and begin there next time. Proceed at a comfortable pace, allowing Timothy to set the agenda.

5. Make a note of any questions you could not answer using the Notes section at the end of each chapter.

6. Pray for your Timothy this week. A phone call or a visit would be an encouragement. When you talk, ask about any concerns that were shared in this session.

Chapter 2: Is the Bible Credible?

The Big Idea: To discover Timothy's thinking and past experiences with the Bible and to invite Timothy to investigate the Bible as a resource for living.

Key Teaching Points

- The Bible is unique and unlike any other book in history.

- The purpose of the Bible is threefold:
    - For God to show Himself to people,
    - To show people how to relate with others,
    - To show people how to interact with God.

- The fulfilled prophecies of the Bible lay a foundation for its credibility.

Teaching Outline

I. What is the Bible?
Published in more languages, and read by more people than any other book, the Bible is actually a library of 66 books, written by 40 writers, on three continents, over a period of 1500 years.

II. Why was the Bible written?
The Bible was written as a means for God to reveal Himself and to set forth principles and illustrations by which we can live and have fellowship with God.

III. Is the Bible credible?
The Bible is credible because the prophecies fulfilled through the life of Christ are beyond chance.

IV. What does the Bible say about itself?
The Bible claims to be "God-breathed" (inspired), useful for teaching, rebuking, correction and training in righteousness.

Page 13:

★ Emphasize these questions from the book.

Q: "Where did you get your view of the Bible?" Is it from your upbringing, a friend, or a memorable experience? Explain.

Q: "On a scale of 1-10, how would you describe your familiarity with the Bible?"

Q: Does historical evidence have value in what you believe?

Ask Timothy specifically about his parents' view of the Bible, church, God, and other questions to discover his spiritual background. We suggest you briefly share your own spiritual background, avoiding "preachy jargon" to facilitate Timothy's responsiveness. The chart on the next page illustrates the layout of the Bible. You may want to print this page for your Timothy.

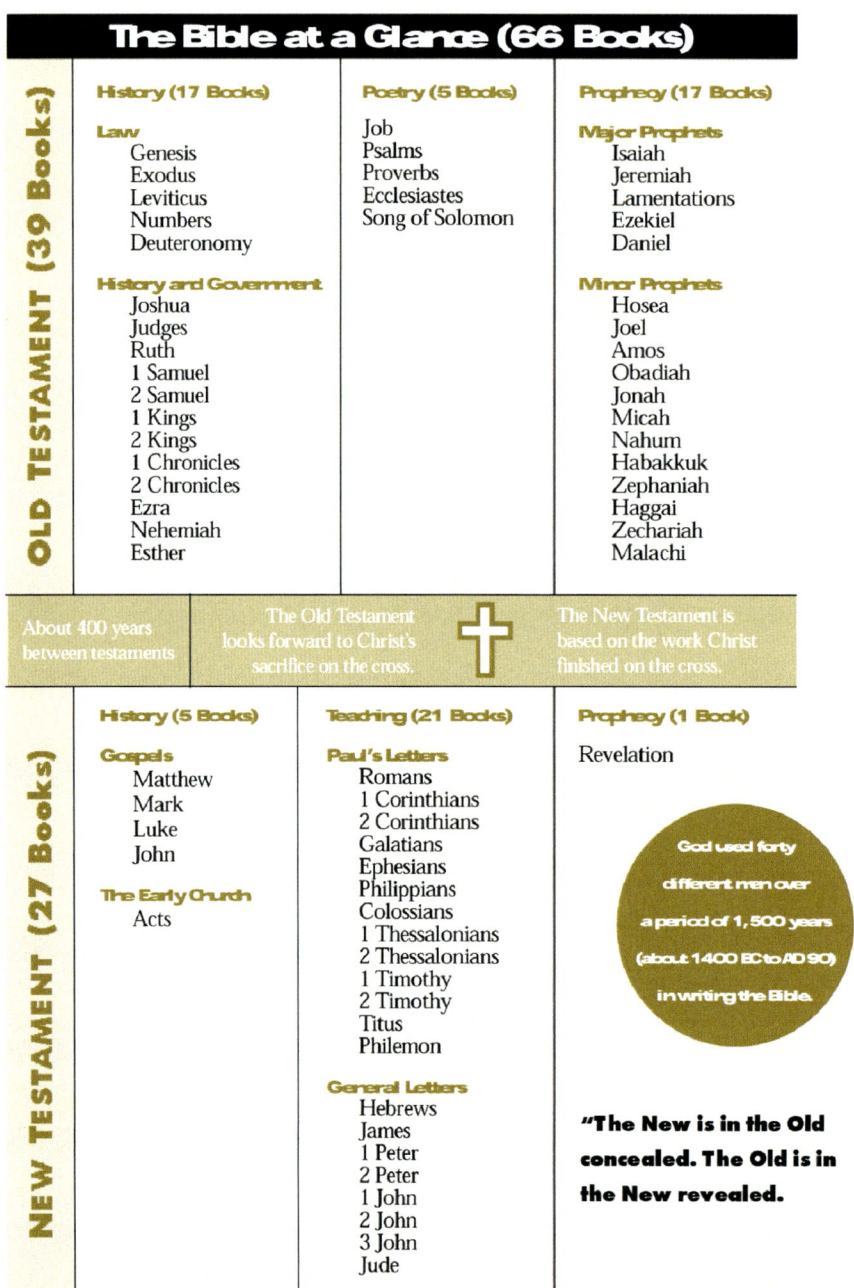

"The New is in the Old concealed. The Old is in the New revealed."

Page 15:

I. What Is the Bible?

Q: What do these mailboxes remind you of? (Our letters from God!)

Notice the quote by Billy Graham on page 16. "Your letters have given me inspiration, quieted my nerves. They bring me so close to you." – Billy to Ruth in 1955.

II. Why Was the Bible Written?

Page 17:

As indicated on page 22 under Additional Resources, please refer to *Evidence That Demands a Verdict* or *The New Evidence That Demands a Verdict* by Josh McDowell. Here are a couple of examples of supporting information from *The New Evidence That Demands a Verdict*, page 38:

The Number of Manuscripts and Their Closeness to the Original:

AUTHOR	BOOK	DATE WRITTEN	EARLIEST COPIES	TIME GAP	NO. OF COPIES
Homer	*Iliad*	800 B.C.	c. 400 B.C.	c. 400 yrs.	643
Herodotus	*History*	480-425 B.C.	c. A.D. 900	c. 1,350 yrs.	8
Thucydides	*History*	460-400 B.C.	c. A.D. 900	c. 1,300 yrs.	8
Plato		400 B.C.	c. A.D. 900	c. 1,300 yrs.	7
Demosthenes		300 B.C.	c. A.D. 1100	c. 1,400 yrs.	200
Caesar	*Gallic Wars*	100-44 B.C.	c. A.D. 900	c. 1,000 yrs.	10
Livy	*History of Rome*	59 B.C.-A.D. 17	4th cent. (partial) mostly 10th cent.	c. 400 yrs. c. 1,000 yrs.	1 partial 19 copies
Tacitus	*Annals*	A.D. 100	c. A.D. 1100	c. 750 yrs.	20
Pliny the Elder	*Natural History*	A.D. 61-113	c. A.D. 850	c. 750 yrs.	7
New Testament		A.D. 50-100	c. 114 (fragment) c. 200 (books) c. 250 (most of N.T.) c. 325 (complete N.T.)	+50 yrs. 100 yrs. 150 yrs. 225 yrs.	5366

Page 18:

Q: What is the significance of some 5,000 ancient Greek copies of the New Testament especially compared to the small number of manuscripts of all other ancient documents?

Page 19:

III. Is the Bible Credible?

Q: What is your reaction to the quote by Hugh Ross the astrophysicist?

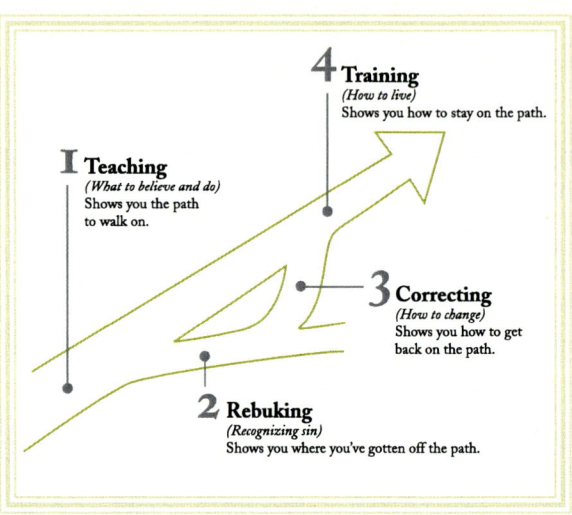

Page 21:

IV. What Does the Bible Say About Itself?

★ Emphasize these questions from the book.

Q: "What are the implications of Paul's claim that the Bible's contents are inspired by God?"

Q: How do you handle correction…do you enjoy it? How do you react?

Q: In what way is God using the Bible in your life today (for teaching, rebuking, etc.)?

Suggestion: Bring a plumbline to your session and use it as you give this illustration.

THE PLUMBLINE: AN ILLUSTRATION

Professional wallpaper hangers constantly use a tool called a "plumbline" or "chalk-line" to ensure wallpaper is hung perfectly straight (If you have a plumbline, you may want have it handy for visual impact). Amateurs, especially first-timers, sometimes fail to see the need for such effort. A friend recently wallpapered a bedroom for her child. Using her plumbline, she carefully hung the first sheet. However, as she progressed around the room, in an effort to conserve time and energy, she used the previous sheet as a guide. About halfway through the job, she stepped back to view her work. It so happened that the paper has a distinctive stripe, which appeared to drift to the left after the second or third sheet and decidedly so at the halfway point. Her efforts to save time had become a costly error.

The Bible refers to itself as a plumbline. When we use it every day and line up our lives with what it says, we stay on course. When we don't, we run the risk of drifting, little by little at first, progressively further and further as we live our lives. In the end, ignoring the Bible's teaching will eventually put us far away from God's standards. That is why a daily visit to God's Word is so important.

Page 22:

Q: How does this picture represent life and religion?

Q: Does the world have many different ways to live or to find purpose in life?

Next Steps

1. Set a day and time to get together again.

2. Encourage your Timothy to consider the Additional Resources, the Optional Applications, and listen to the audio for this chapter on CD or download the message from operationtimothy.com.

3. Assign Chapter 3, "Where is God?" Again, be sensitive. If you did not get through the current chapter, ask Timothy to review it and begin there next time. Proceed at a comfortable pace.

4. Make a note of any questions you could not answer using the Notes section at the end of each chapter.

5. Pray for your Timothy this week. A phone call or a visit would be an encouragement. When you talk, ask about any concerns that were shared in this session.

Chapter 3: Where Is God?

The Big Idea: To discover Timothy's view of God's relevance and to investigate whether God is involved personally in everyday life.

Key Teaching Points:

- His character and instructions about work, relationships, and money demonstrate He is relevant.
- Understanding who God is shows we can trust Him.

Teaching Outline

I. Is God relevant to my life?
   Understanding God's character and instructions about work, relationships and money demonstrate that He is relevant.

II. Can I trust God with my needs?
   We are naturally skeptical because the world tends to say one thing and do another, but God can be trusted because He says so, and has proven it daily throughout history. We can trust God with our lives.

Additional Discussion Questions and Illustrations

As you begin, break the ice with questions about Timothy's week and family. Share some of the highlights of your week as well. You may want to ask additional questions of Timothy to gain more insight into issues or personal matters. For example: "You mentioned last time that you did not grow up in a church. Tell me what Sundays were like for your family."

Page 25:

Q: How would you describe the man in the picture?

Q: Have you ever felt that way? Would you describe when? Why?

What Do People Say?

Q: Which of these quotations is most striking to you? Why?

Take time to understand, to discuss and to ask additional questions regarding Timothy's view of God.

Q: What do you feel has shaped your view of God the most? Why?

Q: Have there been recent events that have changed or altered your understanding in this area? If so, what?

Share from your past or present circumstances and situations that have had an impact on your understanding. Give details on how these experiences are continuing to mold your view of God.

Page 26:

★ Emphasize this question from the book.

Q: To what extent is He involved in your personal life and concerns?

Food for Thought

Page 28:

Q: How do you think this picture might characterize many individual's view of God and faith?

Page 29:

★ Emphasize this question from the book.

Read the quote from Pat Morley's book, *Man in the Mirror* and review the question.

Q: Does Morley's word picture describe you at all? Explain.

Page 30:

God in the Workplace

★ Emphasize these questions from the book.

Allow Timothy to share answers and insights regarding the question:

Q: In your own words, what are the principles God gives about work in Colossians 3:23-25?

If he has not mentioned all of these principles, go back to the passage of Scripture at the top of the page and highlight the principles not mentioned.

1. We are to work wholeheartedly.
2. Our purpose is to please God, not men, in what we do.
3. God says He will reward us.
4. In reality, we are serving Christ.
5. Wrongdoing will be repaid.
6. God shows no favoritism.

Q: How do you think the principles outlined in Colossians apply in any job? Even to the most menial jobs?

Page 31:

God and Relationships

★ Emphasize this question from the book.

Q: How does the quality of your significant relationships compare to this description (in 1 Corinthians 13:4-7)?

The following questions may help develop discussion:

Q: Why are the ideals mentioned in this part of Scripture so difficult for human beings to attain? (The fact is they are impossible without the help of God.)

Q: Can you think of anyone you know, or have heard of, who has measured up to these high standards? (Jesus Christ is the only one to do so.)

Q: What are we to do with these principles? How should they affect our behavior?

Q: Do you think is it possible for us to see these qualities in our lives?

Q: Did you ever carve a heart in a tree? Were you in love? Did you feel you lived up to those ideals as mentioned in 1 Corinthians 13?

Page 32:

God and Your Wallet

Q: Is money good or bad?

Q: In 1 Timothy 6:10, it says that "the love of money is the root of all evil," what do you think that means?

Page 34:

Q: Do you see the father's hand in the right side of the picture? Do you think that the child walking on the bar has greater confidence because the father is there to catch her? How is this like our Father in heaven (see Hebrews 13:8)?

Page 35:

Q: How do you identify with this picture of a tree held in two hands? What does it mean to you?

NOBODY MADE IT: AN ILLUSTRATION

Sir Isaac Newton, famous for his discovery of the law of gravity, once had an atheist friend with whom he had many debates about the existence of God and the reliability of the Scriptures. Frustrated by his inability to communicate, Sir Isaac spent weeks on a project while his friend was out of town. Upon returning from his trip, Sir Isaac's friend visited him. As he entered the room, he was amazed to find an intricate wooden replica of the solar system, with all the planets in relationship to one another. The friend went on and on about the exquisite and precise detail and ingenuity of such a creation.

Finally, he asked Sir Isaac, "Who made such a marvelous model?" Sir Isaac replied, "Nobody made it. It just appeared."

"What?" the friend exclaimed. "Do you take me for a fool? Of course someone made it – stop joking with me and tell me who designed this elaborate, incredible replica of the universe!"

"Nobody made it. It simply appeared one day while you were away." The friend would not accept Sir Isaac' ludicrous explanation, and pressed him again and again to no avail. At last the friend grew angry and demanded, once and for all, a plausible explanation.

Sir Isaac replied: "You are so certain that someone had to have created this very poor imitation of the infinite universe, and yet you assert that the universe itself, a creation far more wondrous than this mere replica, just appeared, without a designer or a creator."

Self-worth Issues?

If you have picked up on self-worth issues in Timothy's life, sharing Psalm 139 may be of help – perhaps even a passage of Scripture to commit to memory or spend time meditating on.

★ Emphasize this question from the book.

Q: "Do you buy it? Why or why not?"

Take time to understand if Timothy accepts that God truly cares for him. Again, here is where you will be able to ascertain whether or not Timothy is grasping the significance of the material. Answers here will give you a better feel for the pace you need to set. Take a few minutes to discuss the responses.

THE WATCHMAKER: AN ANALOGY

William Paley, an 18th century theologian and naturalist, used the following analogy as an apologetic for the existence of God. Paley argued that an earth without a Designer is like finding a watch in the woods. We would not automatically assume that the watch evolved from the rocks, leaves and dirt around it. Instead, we would assume that someone had first designed, then constructed the watch. Why? Because upon examination, we would see the intricate detail and craftsmanship evident in its makeup. Each part has a purpose. Each piece is an integral part of the whole, working with a hundred other pieces for the purpose of producing a means of accurately telling time. If one part is misshapen, the timepiece will not function as it is designed to function.

The earth was created to sustain life. It, like the watch, has a design. Two hundred years after Paley first used his illustration, scientists began identifying precise design specification without which the universe and the earth could not exist. To date, 32 critical design specifications for the earth and 24 for the universe have been identified. If any one of these specifications was altered or missing, the earth would not support life. These discoveries show that the earth has a specific purpose (to provide life) and the earth and the universe were precisely designed to achieve that purpose.

Summary

Since God cares enough about us to provide instructions for us on work, relationships, money and crises in life, He is relevant to life.

Next Steps

1. Set a day and time to get together again.

2. Encourage your Timothy to consider the Additional Resources, the Optional Applications, and listen to the audio for this chapter on CD or at operationtimothy.com.

3. Assign Chapter 4, "Who is Jesus?" Again, be sensitive. If you did not get through the current chapter, ask Timothy to review it and begin there next time. Proceed at a comfortable pace.

4. Make a note of any questions you could not answer using the Notes section at the end of each chapter.

5. Pray for your Timothy this week. A phone call or a visit would be an encouragement. When you talk, ask about any concerns that were shared in this session.

Chapter 4: Who Is Jesus?

The Big Idea: To encourage Timothy to consider the evidence for Jesus' humanity as well as His deity.

Key Teaching Points

- Jesus entered time and space 2000 years ago as a man. He walked, talked, ate, slept, got hungry, died on a cross, was buried, and rose from the dead.
- Jesus was more than a good man or a great teacher; He was God. The testimony of His disciples, the miracles He performed, and what Jesus said about Himself confirm His deity.

Teaching Outline

I. Jesus' Humanity
Jesus experienced and understood suffering, temptation, and death so that we could relate to Him.

II. Jesus' Deity
Jesus was the promised Messiah.
Jesus' deity was revealed to His disciples.
Jesus' deity gave Him all authority and power over nature, to forgive sin and raise people from the dead.

Additional Discussion Questions and Illustrations

Be sure to cover all Scriptures, either reading aloud or sharing how you both answered the questions. Keep asking, "What does this mean to you?" or "What do you hear in this verse?"

Jesus' Humanity

Page 39:

Read the section, "What Do People Say?" and ask for reactions.

★ Emphasize these questions from the book.

Q: Which of these thoughts captures your perception of Jesus?

Q: Who do you believe Jesus is?

Page 40:

There are many differing views of Jesus--spawning quite a few struggles. Here are some examples. Some see him as a moral or ethical teacher, ignoring some of the difficult things he said in favor of ideas such as loving your neighbors and building with solid foundations. Some see him as a social revolutionary, preaching justice and equality in the face of oppression. Some see him as one of many prophets, unique but not a final Word from God. Some people, believing that spiritual things are completely separate from physical things, suggest a great spirit inhabited Jesus, the man, for his time in ministry and left him before he died.

chapter 4 - who is Jesus?

Page 44:

★ Emphasize this question from the book.

Q: What would you say about Jesus?

INSIGHT ABOUT HIGH PRIEST

The reference on page 44, Hebrews 4:14-15, refers to Jesus being our high priest. It is important for your Timothy to understand the role of the high priest in the temple in order to realize how Jesus intercedes for us. On the Day of Atonement, as described in Leviticus 16:1-32, the high priest made a sin-offering for his sins and the sins of the entire nation. This offering was made in the Holy of Holies of the temple, where the Ark of the Covenant resided. To prepare for this day, the high priest had to purify himself both spiritually and physically, and if any part of this ritual was flawed, it was believed that he would not return from the Holy of Holies alive. Therefore, the task of the high priest was to usher men into the presence of God and to offer the sacrifice for the sins of his people to God on the Day of Atonement. To be a perfect high priest, He would have to know God perfectly and know men perfectly. Jesus, as both God and man, fulfilled this role perfectly. As it says in Hebrews 4:15, believers have Jesus as our high priest, a man like us in every way, but without sin. Jesus brought God and man together in His own form and continues to bring them together by faith.

Page 46:

Q: What does it mean to you that Jesus experienced hunger, fatigue, thirst – do you think He can sympathize without weaknesses?

Jesus' Deity

Q: Are you familiar with John the Baptist? Elijah? Jeremiah? Why would people think Jesus was one of them?

Page 47:

★ Emphasize this question from the book – from the passage, Matthew 16:13-17

Q: What did Jesus claim about Himself?

★ Emphasize this question from the book – From the passage, John 10:30-33

Q: Were the Jews justified for being offended by Jesus' words? Why or why not?

BK1:31

Q: What is your reaction to Jesus' claim?

Spiritual Background

Your Timothy may raise questions here about eternal life. Chapters 5 and 6 of *Operation Timothy* deal with this subject in detail. The point here is the Jew's reaction to Jesus' claims of being the Messiah, i.e. if He were merely claiming to be a prophet or a great teacher, they would not have had such a violent response.

Note: Whatever your Timothy's response to the question of Jesus' claim, accept where he is, and continue to ask why he feels this way. This will give insight into Timothy's obstacles to belief and perhaps some hurts from the past. Invite him to continue investigating Scripture with you before drawing conclusions.

Read Matthew 14:22-33 aloud.

> Q: What is happening as we pick up the story?
>
> Q: Why do you think Jesus sought to be alone?
>
> Q: Have you ever felt "buffeted by the waves"? In what way?
>
> Q: Jesus said, "It is I." "In your opinion, why was this good news to them?"
>
> Q: At what point did Peter begin to sink?
>
> Q: How might this story apply to our lives today?

Next Steps

1. Set a day and time to get together again.

2. Encourage your Timothy to consider the Additional Resources, the Optional Applications, and listen to the audio for this chapter on CD or at operationtimothy.com.

3. Assign Chapter 5, "Why did Jesus come?" Again, be sensitive. If you did not get through the current chapter, ask Timothy to review it and begin there next time. Proceed at a comfortable pace.

4. Make a note of any questions you could not answer using the Notes section at the end of each chapter.

5. Pray for your Timothy this week. A phone call or a visit would be an encouragement. When you talk, ask about any concerns that were shared in this session.

Chapter 5: Why Did Jesus Come?

The Big Idea: To allow Timothy to discover why Jesus came to earth, why and how He died, was raised to life and to establish the fact that He is coming again.

Key Teaching Points

- Jesus came to provide the way for man to have a relationship with God.
- Jesus did many miracles to demonstrate that He was more than a mere man.
- Jesus died by crucifixion, and He rose from the dead.
- Jesus will come again in the final days of the earth.

Teaching Outline

I. Why did Jesus Christ come?
    Jesus came to save us from our sins.

II. What did Jesus do?
    Jesus led a life to be imitated, was the most influential teacher in history, offered hope to the outcasts of society, and demonstrated power over disease, nature, and even death.

III. Why and how did Jesus die?
    He did not die because He had done anything wrong.
    He knew in advance that He would be crucified, but He went to Jerusalem anyway.
    He suffered and died to bring us peace with God.
    He died for you.

IV. Did Jesus rise again?
    Jesus' resurrection is a key to faith. Over 500 eyewitnesses, including all the disciples and later the Apostle Paul, saw Jesus alive after his death.

V. What else is left for Jesus to do?
    The Bible says He will soon come again to take those who believe in Him.

Page 51:

Q: What is your reaction to a phone call when you don't know the purpose or reason for the call?

Page 53:

Why Did Jesus Christ Come?

★ Emphasize this question from the book. Spend some time with Timothy going over the verses outlined on page 53.

Q: Why did Jesus come?

Page 54:

What did Jesus do?

Q: How does this picture capture the points made by Gregory of Nazianzus?

Miracles

If Timothy is not familiar with most of the miracles, take time to read a few together. If he is interested, note the reference below for further study:

> **Healing:**
> Lepers cleansed: Matthew 8:3; Luke 17:14
> Paralytic healed: Mark 2:3-12
> Nobleman's son: John 4:46-53
> Withered hand: Matthew 12:10-13
>
> **Nature:**
> Water to wine: John 2:6-10
> Quieted storm: Matthew 8:23-26; Matthew 14:32
> Huge fish catch: Luke 5:4-6; John 21:6
> Walk on water: Matthew 14:25-27
>
> **Power over Life:**
> Jairus' daughter: Matthew 9:18-26; Mark 5:22-43; Luke 8:41-56
> Widow's son: Luke 7:12-15

Page 55:

★ Emphasize this question from the book on page 55.

Q: "According to the adjacent passages, what was Jesus' purpose for performing miracles?"

Page 57:

Why and How Did Jesus Die?

INSIGHT

No other passage of Scripture so vividly portrays the death of Jesus Christ and communicates the sacrifice He made on our behalf as does Isaiah 53. Dedicate one of your quiet times this week to read and meditate on this passage.

Q: Isaiah 53:5-6–In your opinion, how are we like the sheep mentioned in this passage? Why?

Q: Romans 5:8–What is the difference between saying you love someone and proving it? What's the significance of Christ dying for us "while we were still sinners"?

Definitions for some of the key words in the verses at the top of page 57:

Vine's Expository Dictionary of Old and New Testament Words defines…

> **Transgressions**: Primarily a going aside, then, an overstepping of the prescribed limit.
>
> **Iniquity**: Lawlessness or wickedness or unrighteousness; "a condition of not being right, whether with God, according the standard of His holiness and righteousness, or with man according to the standard of what man knows to be right by his conscience."
>
> **Sin**: a missing of the mark (as in an archer aiming for the goal with his bow and missing the bulls-eye or even the whole board); wrongdoing.
>
> **Justify**: To acquit from guilt.

Your Timothy may raise questions about how a loving God could be so harsh. One way to address this is to also communicate that while He is a loving God, He is also a fair and just judge.

Death by Crucifixion

It may be well to remind ourselves of what death by crucifixion meant in the thoughts of the ancient world. With the passing of the years, Christendom has cast a halo of beauty round the cross… But all this ought not to hide from us the fact that originally the cross was a thing unspeakably shameful and degrading… Devised in the first instance in semi-barbaric Oriental lands, death by crucifixion was reserved by the Romans for slaves and for criminals of the most abandoned kind.

> James Stewart, *The Life and Teaching of Jesus Christ*

Judge for Yourself: A Story

> The gavel came down. Guilty! The judge looked down at the defendant.
>
> "Young man, do you understand that you committed a crime and must now pay the consequences?" The boy nodded without looking up.
>
> "As an upholder of the law, I must see that justice is served. That's irreversible," said the judge slowly. Then after a pause, he unbuttoned his black robe. "However, I can take the prisoner's punishment for him."
>
> The prosecutor looked up sharply. "What kind of judge would do that?"
>
> The judge replied, "One who is the prisoner's father."

Timothy may not understand the significance of the bread and the wine as representing Christ's death on the cross. If this is new to him, read Luke 22:19-20, "And He took bread, gave thanks and broke [it], and gave [it] to them, saying, 'This is My body which is given for you; do this in remembrance of Me.' Likewise He also [took] the cup after supper, saying, 'This cup [is] the new covenant in My blood, which is shed for you.'

Page 58:

Did Jesus Rise Again?

If Timothy has doubts about the resurrection, don't attempt to answer all doubts and questions. Keep asking questions such as…

Q: How old were you when you first began to doubt? What did your parents believe? Were there others in your life who influenced your view?

Page 59:

Read aloud the caption under the map. In addition to the question posed in the caption, ask the following:

Q: When did the disciples believe the Scripture and the words that Jesus had spoken? Why do you think this is significant?

★ Emphasize this question from the book.

Q: According to the verses above, why is Christ's resurrection so important?

When Jesus was taken away to die, his small handful of followers scattered and hid. Within a few years, the Christian faith had overtaken no less than the Roman empire, and those original followers had become willing to face execution themselves. How can we account for these actions without a well-attested resurrection?

What Else Is Left for Jesus to Do?

Encouraging Words

Paul tells us to "encourage each other with these words" in 1 Thessalonians 4:15-18. Discuss why these words should be a comfort to us today…

Three final items in God's plan:

1. Jesus is coming soon.
2. He is bringing His reward with Him.
3. He will give to everyone according to what he has done.

Final Thoughts

Take time to talk through what impressed you both from this study. Don't attempt to convince, debate, or persuade at this point. Encourage Timothy to spend time reviewing the Scriptures, thinking, and praying about its significance in his life.

Next Steps

1. Set a day and time to get together again.

2. Encourage your Timothy to consider the Additional Resources, the Optional Applications, and listen to the audio for this chapter on CD or at operationtimothy.com.

3. Assign Chapter 6, "Can I be Accepted and Forgiven?" Again, be sensitive. If you did not get through the current chapter, ask Timothy to review it and begin there next time. Proceed at a comfortable pace.

4. Make a note of any questions you could not answer using the Notes section at the end of each chapter.

5. Pray for your Timothy this week. A phone call or a visit would be an encouragement. When you talk, ask about any concerns that were shared in this session.

NOTES

Chapter 6: Can I Be Accepted and Forgiven?

The Big Idea: To allow Timothy to discover how to be forgiven and gain a relationship with God without forcing a decision on the spot.

Key Teaching Points

- No one is perfect. All have sinned and are separated from God.
- We all need forgiveness.
- The basis for forgiveness is not what we do (i.e. good works), but receiving what Jesus has done for us.
- Forgiveness is a gift, but it must be received.
- The result is that we are no longer condemned, but have peace with God.

Teaching Outline

I. Making forgiveness personal
   We struggle with forgiveness in business and in our personal relationships.

II. Do we need forgiveness?
   We need forgiveness from God because our sin has separated us from Him.

III. What is the basis for forgiveness?
   Jesus Christ's death on the cross is offered as a substitute for the punishment we deserve.

Definition of Forgiveness

Vine's Dictionary of Old and New Testament Words defines…

> Forgive: to send forth, to send away, denoting a dismissal, a release of debts or sins, as being completely canceled.

Page 63:

★ Emphasize this question from the book.

Q: "Why is forgiveness so important to the human experience?

Read aloud and discuss the quote on page 64 by Lewis Smedes, the author of *Forgive and Forget*. As additional background, here is more of what Mr. Smedes wrote in *Forgive and Forget*, pp. 169-170:

> Forgiveness offers a chance at reconciliation; it is an opportunity for a life together instead of death together. Forgiveness is a miracle of the will that moves away the heavy hindrance to fellowship, a miracle that will be fulfilled when the two estranged people come together in as fair a new relationship as is possible at that time and under those circumstances.
>
> The alternative to reconciliation is, in the end, a ceaseless process of self-destruction. The brilliant American theologian Reinhold Neibuhr saw this after World War II and said: "We must finally be reconciled with our foe, lest we both perish in the vicious circle of hatred." There must be a release from the past, or we are forever grounded on its unfair pain.

Vengeance never wholly satisfies. For one thing, we are not always able to fight back. Maybe the person who hurt us is dead. Maybe we are old and weak. What is left to us then but our private truculence? . . . When you suspect that forgiving is not fair, you worry that the people who hurt you are not getting what is coming to them. But you worry, too, that you are getting a bad deal; you get hurt and do not get even. . . . Forgiving is the only way to be fair to yourself. Getting even is a loser's game. . . . Recall the pain of being wronged, the hurt of being stung, cheated, demeaned. Doesn't the memory of it fuel the fire of fury again, reheat the pain again, make it hurt again? Suppose you never forgive . . . you have become a prisoner of your past pain; you are locked into a torture chamber of your own making. Time should have left your pain behind; but you keep it alive to let it flay you over and over. . . . The only way to heal the pain that will not heal itself is to forgive the person who hurt you. Forgiving stops the reruns of pain. Forgiving heals your memory as you change your memory's vision.

> "As it is written: 'There is no one righteous, not even one; there is... no one who seeks God.'"
>
> Romans 3:10, 11
>
> "...for all have sinned and fall short of the glory of God."
>
> Romans 3:23
>
> "Therefore, just as sin entered the world through one man, and death through sin, and in this way death came to all men, because all sinned."
>
> Romans 5:12

What We Need Is Forgiveness

Page 65:

★ Emphasize this question from the book.

Q: Why does forgiveness trigger such a powerful response in people?

Making Forgiveness Personal

Page 67:

Do We Need Forgiveness?

As you go through these verses with your Timothy, have him read a verse aloud and then you read a verse aloud and underline key words.

Page 68:

In these three verses, we see that man is separated from God by his sin – wanting to go his own way. Use the diagram on page 68 to emphasize this separation – you may want to have Timothy write this across the illustration on the "gap."

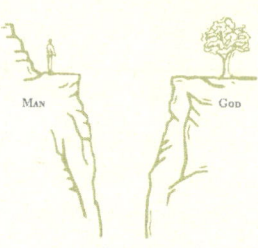

What Is the Basis for Forgiveness?

Q: Isaiah 53:6 says that we are "like sheep, that have gone astray, each of us has turned to his own way." Do you agree? Explain.

Page 69:

Discuss the sensitive subject of good works with Timothy. Use this to lead into the diagram – "We try to do the right things to get to God…"

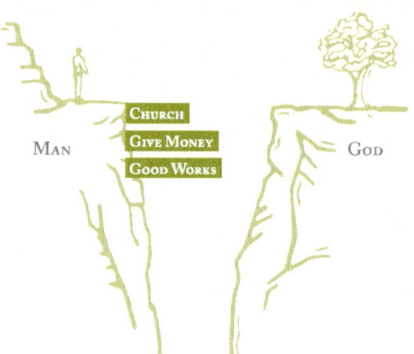

Titus 3:5 says, "He saved us not because of the righteous things we have done, but because of His mercy."

Q: What does this say about what God is providing for us? What does this mean to you personally?

Read Ephesians 2:8-9 aloud.

Q: Why does the Bible say God won't accept our works as a payment for sin?

Page 70:

Read John 5:24 (on page 71), "I tell you the truth, whoever hears my word and believes him who sent me has eternal life and will not be condemned; he has crossed over from death to life."

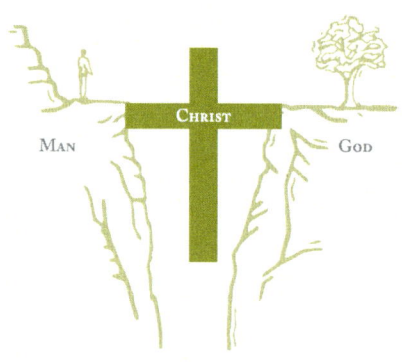

Have your Timothy write in the words, "Hear" and "Believe" from John 5:24 above the cross on the diagram. Then write the three results of this choice, "eternal life, no condemnation, from death to life," under the tree and the word "God."

★ Emphasize this question from the book.

Q: How can one receive this forgiveness?

Receiving a Gift: An Illustration

Let's say I was going to give you this pen as a gift. My part is to offer it to you. What is your part? You must receive it. Only then is it actually in your possession (go through the motions as you talk).

Ask Timothy to read from his/her response to this question on how to receive God's forgiveness. Be discerning at this point. If there is resistance, move on. If there is willingness, say something like: "Let's pray together. Remember, God is not as interested in your words as He is in the attitude of your heart…" If Timothy is unsure how to pray, offer your help by praying a phrase at a time, asking Timothy to follow.

I know I am a sinner, and need Your forgiveness.
I believe that Jesus Christ died for my sins.
I am willing to turn from my sins.
I now invite Jesus Christ to come into my heart and life as my personal Savior.
I am willing, by God's strength, to follow and obey Jesus Christ as the Lord of my life.

Page 71:

★ Emphasize this question from the book on the top of page 71.

Q: What is meant by crossing from death to life? Is this literal or metaphorical? Explain.

Next Steps

1. Set a day and time to get together again.

2. Give Timothy *Life Foundations* (Book 2) and assign Chapter 1.

3. Open *Life Foundations* and go over the table of contents. Timothy will need a Bible for this study, and there is a memory verse for each chapter. As a Paul, you need to know if Timothy has a Bible. If not, suggest that an NIV (New International Version) would be best because the study is based on it. Point out the perforated cards at the end of the book. Share a brief faith story of how memorizing Scripture has helped you in your Christian life.

4. Encourage your Timothy to consider the Additional Resources, the Optional Applications, and listen to the audio for this chapter on CD or at operationtimothy.com.

5. Make a note of any questions you could not answer using the Notes section at the end of each chapter.

6. Pray for your Timothy this week. A phone call or a visit would be an encouragement. When you talk, ask about any concerns that were shared in this session.

leader's guide for book 2
LIFE FOUNDATIONS
SUGGESTED DISCUSSIONS AND QUESTIONS

Chapter 1: New Life in Christ

The Big Idea: To demonstrate that every believer can know for certain they have eternal life and begin to enjoy the benefits of that life today.

Key Teaching Points

- Jesus Christ is the only way to eternal life. All we can do is surrender our lives to His control and accept His free gift of salvation resulting in eternal life.

- We have a connection with God through Christ by believing, confessing, and repenting of our sins.

- We can be sure about our eternal destiny.

- Eternal life begins now, not in heaven someday.

Teaching Outline

I. Made that Way
From the moment we were created, we were spiritual beings and intended for a relationship with God. We were made to need God.

II. The Source of Eternal Life
Our source of eternal life is God reaching down to us through Jesus Christ.

III. Gaining Eternal Life
Through repentance and faith we receive eternal life.

IV. Believe, Confess, and Repent

V. I'm So Sure
We can know that we have eternal life because of Scripture.

Open with the *That's What They Say* and discuss the story of Mel Fisher, "Buried Treasure," and what real lasting treasure is.

Preparation for the Leader

If Timothy has not prepared for the lesson ahead of time, take a few moments to discuss and discern the situation: Lack of time? Difficulty locating the books of the Bible? Be sensitive to the fact that it may take a while for Timothy to become adept at locating Scripture references.

You may want to work through the lesson together, looking up verses, filling in blanks, etc. Another approach would be to take a week to review the table of contents of the Bible. Have Timothy turn to a couple of books, pointing out the New and the Old Testament and how the books are arranged by chapter and verse.

Page 1:

Q: Did you ever look for a treasure?

Page 2:

I. Made that Way

As Timothy answers the questions on the top of page 3, you may want to share a couple of quotes. Pascal has been quoted as saying that "man was created with a God-size vacuum." Here's the actual quote:

> "What else does this craving, and this helplessness, proclaim but that there was once in man a true happiness, of which all that now remains is the empty print and trace? This he tries in vain to fill with everything around him, seeking in things that are not there the help he cannot find in those that are, though none can help, since this infinite abyss can be filled only with an infinite and immutable object; in other words by God himself." – Blaise Pascal

Here's what Solomon said, "He (God) has put eternity in their hearts…" (Ecclesiastes 3:11).

Page 4:

Q: This section is called "Made That Way." Do you believe that you were made with a

spiritual need? Why or why not?

Page 5:

Q: How are we like a child holding on to his father's finger?

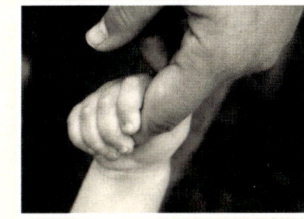

II. The Source of Eternal Life

Q: What comes to your mind when the term "eternal life" is used?

Page 7:

As you discuss 1 Peter 3:18, you may want to refer back to the illustration on page 70 of *Life Questions* (or draw it on a napkin), that shows how Christ Jesus "brings us to God."

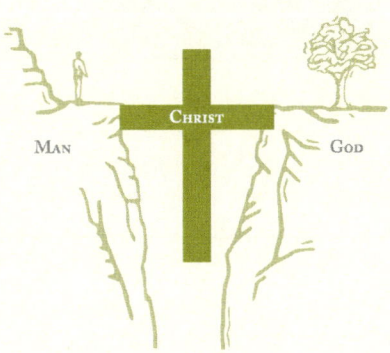

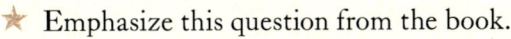 Emphasize this question from the book.

Q: Examine John 17:3. Jesus claims that He is the source of eternal life. What do you think knowing Him looks like?

> In the verse, the word "know" in the Greek is the same word that is used in Genesis 4:17, 25 and Matthew 1:25, where the term refers to an intimacy between a man and a woman. Eternal life is life in the here and now where we have a close, personal relationship with God.

Page 8:

III. Gaining Eternal Life

Receiving the Gift

Q: Other religions teach their own ways to God. What are your thoughts about ways to God?

Here's a point which may come up in this discussion. When talking about various religions, Ravi Zacharias often notes that all the major religions have their exclusivity. Even if they seem to teach that many ways can go to heaven, dig deep enough and you'll see they insist you believe certain doctrines to properly understand spiritual life, such as the law of karma or the authority of certain teachers. All major religions will reach this point, a claim similar to what the Romans wanted from the early church. They said they had no problem with early Christians worshipping Jesus as God, but they must worship Caesar as the highest god too. All roads could reach god, they said, if only you believed as they believed.

Page 9:

IV. Believe, Confess, and Repent

Q: Was the decision to believe in Christ out of your comfort zone? Explain how?

Vine's Dictionary of Old and New Testament Words defines...

> Repentance: Literally, to perceive afterwards, signifying a change of one's mind or purpose, always in the New Testament involving change for the better, an amendment, and always of... repentance from sin, and this change of mind involves both a turning from sin and a turning to God.

 a

The parable of the prodigal son is an outstanding illustration of this. Christ began His ministry with a call to repentance (Matthew 4:17). The call is addressed to the individual.

Page 10:

V. I'm So Sure

Q: In what way(s) have you experienced the kind of life Jesus is talking about in John 10:10? What do you struggle with that keeps you from experiencing the abundant life?

Page 11:

Hooked on a Feeling - Together

Q: What are your feelings: antagonistic, receptive, skeptical, hungry, or puzzled?

Q: Is there something from your background or previous experience that you are having difficulty overcoming?

If Timothy has been taught that a person can lose his salvation, this lesson may be difficult. Questions may surface regarding certain Scripture references. Be aware that even if there is acceptance of the assurance of eternal life, there still may be times in which Timothy struggles emotionally with this issue. Be patient. Don't try to debate and persuade, but speak the truth with love as best you can.

Note: If Timothy has suffered abandonment from a parent or close family member, he/she may grapple with the feeling that God could also abandon him. Encourage Timothy to memorize 1 John 5:11-13 and meditate on it often. If you find the need to recommend more verses, try John 6:46-47, 11:25-26, and Romans 6:22-23.

Page 12:

Here Today, God's Tomorrow

Q: In Scripture, it says, "No eye has seen, no ear has heard, no mind has conceived what God has prepared for those who love him" (1 Corinthians 2:9). However, we know some things now, so how does the light shining through the trees in this picture illustrate how wonderful eternal life will be?

Scripture Memory Verse: New Life in Christ

Don't skip this section. Even if you personally have difficulty memorizing Scripture, ask God to help you in the process as you help Timothy. Remember: you must memorize if you expect Timothy to. It's critical for growth. Every person who has devoted the time and effort to this one discipline says that nothing else benefits them as greatly. Peace, lifestyle changes, reassurance, joy, character development: these are but a few of the rewards of memorizing and meditating on Scripture.

Q: "How does this Scripture Memory Verse capture the key point of this lesson?"

Cover pages 12 and 13 thoroughly with Timothy. Share your own experiences, good and bad.

NOTES

> REMINDER: Operation Timothy is based on Paul's instruction to young Timothy in 2 Timothy 2:2, "And the things you have heard me say in the presence of many witnesses entrust to reliable men who will also be qualified to teach others."
>
> Suggest to your "Timothy" that he begin praying about a man that he may disciple.

INCRIMINATING EVIDENCE
A True Story by Olive Bishop Branch

It was October of 1806. Three weeks before, Napoleon's armies had defeated Prussia at the battle of Jena. The myth of Prussian invincibility has been shattered and the conqueror was in Berlin, determined to exact an enormous tribute from the conquered.

It was at this time that the Prince of Hatzfeld was arrested, a proven traitor to Napoleon. The death warrant was signed and the prince was thrown in prison to await his execution. The wife of the prince was convinced of his innocence. She sat in the street outside the Emperor's headquarters for hours, waiting to see him. When he finally came, she threw herself at his feet and pleaded with tears for the life of her husband, basing her plea upon her firm belief in her husband's innocence.

Napoleon said nothing but turned his piercing eyes upon her. The silence was awesome. Finally Talleyrand handed him a letter which he in turn gave to the weeping princess. She read it eagerly. "Whose writing is that, Madame?" Napoleon asked.

The princess dropped the paper. "Is that not your husband's handwriting?" The princess only sobbed. She had recognized the signature.

For one of the few times recorded in his career, Napoleon showed compassion. He asked Talleyrand, "Do we have other evidence against the Prince of Hatzfeld?" "No" was the answer.

Turning to the weeping princess, the Emperor said, "Put the letter in the fire, and then we will have no evidence against your husband." As the letter burned to ashes, all the evidence of treason against the Prince of Hatzfeld was destroyed forever.

Rarely did Napoleon show a forgiving spirit, but God is continually merciful and forgiving on the basis of the sacrifice of His Son. By faith in Him, the evidence against us is destroyed forever and we may stand before God justified, as though we had never sinned.

Next Steps

1. Review 1 John 5:11-13. Encourage Timothy to go over this verse daily as he begins to memorize 2 Corinthians 5:17.

2. Encourage your Timothy to consider the Additional Resources, the Optional Applications, and listen to the audio for this chapter on CD or at operationtimothy.com. In this audio CD, Howard Hendricks defines the Christian Life as "the life of Christ reproduced in the believer by the power of the Holy Spirit in obedient response to the Word of God."

3. Assign chapter 2, "Our New Identify." Point out the memory verse card in the back of the book. Write down date, time, and place for the next session.

4. Update your diary and pray for your Timothy this week.

Chapter 2: Our New Identity

The Big Idea: To begin an exploration of the depths of our identity in Christ and to realize that God has given us everything to live the Christian life.

Key Teaching Points

- The world will attempt to define who I am, but it is more important to know who God says I am.
- We receive a new identity at the moment of salvation – new creation, new family, and new heritage.
- We live the Christian life as we abide in a relationship with Jesus Christ.

Teaching Outline

I. Who Am I in God's Eyes?
   It is much more important to know who God says I am than for me to define who I am. When we trust in Christ, we are adopted into God's family; therefore, we have a new identity, a new heritage, and a new future. The Christian life is not a matter of trying to do things for God, but claiming and resting in what He has done for us.

II. What Does This Mean to Me?
   When we are spiritually reborn, we are instantly changed from being a sinner, who is an enemy of God, to being forgiven, a friend of God, and in fact, a beloved child of the King!

III. How Do I Live This Way?
   We can only live the Christian life as we abide in our relationship with Jesus Christ.

IV. Power for Living
   Christ in us is the power to live the Christian life, and it is a process of transformation in which we are progressively conformed to the image of Christ.

Page 17: Define Self

Q: Have you asked yourself, "Who am I?" What measure do you use for identity? Success? Appearance? Personal History? Background?

Understanding who we are in Christ is a key point for Timothy to grasp. Read the last paragraph on page 17 and get his reaction to the emphasized sentence. Don't try to force Timothy to accept this statement, but revisit it at the end of the chapter.

> If I am defined by the One who made me and owns me, it makes sense to look back to Him for clues about who I am. *It is much more important to know who God says I am than for me to define who I am.* Knowing who we are before attempting to live life by doing something is essential to being fulfilled, being at peace with yourself and living in harmony with others. In other words it is "Who before Do."

I. Who Am I in God's Eyes?

Page 19:

★ Emphasize the three questions from the book on page 19.

Q: What do these verses communicate to you about your acceptance?

Q: How do Romans 8:1-2 and Romans 8:28 give you a sense of security?

Q: How significant are you in God's eyes?

Page 20:

Who I Am in Christ

Take turns reading aloud the descriptions of being "accepted," "secure," and "significant" and looking up any of the verses that are surprising to your Timothy.

Page 22:

II. What Does This Mean to Me?

Q: On what basis are you part of a family? Is it because of what you do?

★ Note: Be careful here. Many people struggle with seeing God as a father and seeing themselves as His child because of the experiences with their father. Be sensitive to this point to use Scripture to define how God as a perfect Father loves and care for us.

Page 23:

Verses that support the descriptions on the top of page 23:

- From an enemy of God to a friend of God - James 4:4,
- From a child of Satan to a child of God – John 8:44,
- From being not accepted by God to being fully accepted by God – Acts 15:8,
- From being guilty to being forgiven – Ephesians 1:7,
- From being condemned to receiving a full pardon – Isaiah 55:7,
- From being opposed by God to being the apple of His eye – Psalms 17:8,
- From being totally unlovely to being lovely and lovable – John 14:21,
- From being a commoner to being royalty – Matthew 25:34,
- From being a sinner to being a saint – Ephesians 2:19.

⭐ Emphasize this question from the book.

Q: If what the above statements say about the new you are accurate, what actual difference does that make to you?

Page 25:

⭐ Emphasize this question from the book.

Be sure to reflect on the quote by Ken Boa, particularly the last paragraph and the question at the bottom of the page.

Q: How do these thoughts impact you personally?

Page 26:

Q: Do you accept these statements in the summary to be true for your life? Which of these seven statements are most meaningful to you?

III. How Do I Live This Way?

Read John 15:4-5 together.

Q: What does abide mean in this passage? Who is the branch and who is the vine in this botanical analogy? (Note: abide – to remain or stay around)

Page 27:

⭐ Emphasize this question from the book.

Q: Our own strength is never strong enough. How does the implication of that statement affect you?

Page 29:

IV. Power for Living

Have your Timothy read the quote by C. S. Lewis from *Mere Christianity*.

Q: Do you understand what a paradox is? (Definition: a statement or proposition that seems self-contradictory or absurd but in reality expresses a possible truth.)

Q: What are some of C.S. Lewis' paradoxes given to the left of this picture in the book?

Here are some examples of paradoxes to discuss with Timothy:

"Your real, new self will not come as long as you are looking for it."

"Lose your life, and you will save it."

"Only the things you have given away will ever really be yours."

"Only the dead can be resurrected."

Spend some time on the observations about our indwelling, which is "Christ in Me" (center of page 29), and look up the verses associated with each statement.

It is important for Timothy to understand that the Christian life involves a process of transformation in which we are progressively conformed to the image of Christ. In future lessons of *Operation Timothy*, this will become clearer, but it is important that Timothy not become discouraged if his life is not suddenly and dramatically changed.

Page 30:

Memory Verse: Our New Identity

Q: How does this Scripture Memory Verse capture the key point of this lesson?

Next Steps

1. Set a day and time to get together again.

2. Encourage your Timothy to consider the Additional Resources, the Optional Applications, and listen to the audio for this chapter on CD or at operationtimothy.com and consider watching The *Jesus* Film with your spouses.

3. Assign Chapter 3, "Battling the World, the Flesh and the Devil."

4. Make a note of any questions you could not answer using the Notes section at the end of each chapter.

5. Update your diary and pray for your Timothy this week.

NOTES

> REMINDER: Operation Timothy is based on Paul's instruction to young Timothy in 2 Timothy 2:2, "And the things you have heard me say in the presence of many witnesses entrust to reliable men who will also be qualified to teach others."
>
> Suggest to your "Timothy" that he begin praying about a man that he may disciple.

Chapter 3: Battling the World, the Flesh and the Devil

The Big Idea: To forewarn and forearm Timothy with the knowledge that our enemy, Satan, is real and desires to shipwreck our lives.

Key Teaching Points

- We are in a spiritual battle that is unseen and supernatural in nature.
- This spiritual battle is with the world, the flesh, and the devil.
- Satan and his forces are extremely clever, subtle, and powerful.
- God has not left us defenseless but provides spiritual armor.
- Because of what Christ did on the cross to defeat death, Satan's most powerful weapon, the final outcome has been decided.

Teaching Outline

I. What is the spiritual battle?
   This is not a battle of man against man or nation against nation. This is an unseen battle of a supernatural dimension against several enemies – the world, the flesh, and Satan. We don't use guns and missiles in this spiritual battle, but it is nonetheless very real.

II. What is the battle with the world?
   There are many things in this world that can distract us and lure our hearts away from Christ. When we buy into the world's standards of wealth, prestige, and position, we are subtly drawn away from the freedom and joy that we can experience in Christ.

III. What is the battle with the flesh?
   When we become Christians, we have a new "inner man," but the "old man" is still at work in our bodies causing conflict. These old appetites, attitudes, memories, and habits can surface at any time and wage war against the life of Christ in us. This conflict remains with us until we die or Christ returns.

IV. What is the battle with Satan?
   Satan is the prince of this world and extremely clever, subtle, and powerful. He deceived Eve and attempted to snare Christ, but God has determined the final outcome, and final victory is assured because of what Christ did on the cross.

V. How do we have victory?
   We have victory by being vigilant, resisting the devil, memorizing and obeying God's Word, and depending on the Holy Spirit.

Page 33:

Dirty Business

Q: Do you feel like you are in a war in this Christian life?

Page 36:

Q: How does spiritual warfare seem real to you?

Page 38:

II. What Is the Battle with the World?

Q: What are the things that you struggle with?

Page 39:

★ Emphasize these questions from the book.

Q: Look at 1 John 2:15-17. What are the three elements of the world that we struggle with?

Q: It has been said, "It is not what you possess, it's what possesses you." Do you agree with this statement?

Q: Where does the struggle occur – internally or externally?

III. What Is the Battle with the Flesh?

The word "flesh" is used in the New Testament to describe our physical bodies, humanity in general, and sinful cravings – those things that are contrary to God's will. In this context, it is dealing with the sinful desires that can overwhelm us.

Discuss the applications of the Scripture passages at the top of page 41.

Page 41:

IV. What Is the Battle with Satan?

Q: "How do you visualize Satan?"

Read this aloud to Timothy:

> Devil of a time--The "prince of this world" has his day in the sun. He causes human pain and wages war against the Creator who cast him out of heaven long ago, but God has written the last word and already announced his fate. Jesus neutralized Satan's ultimate weapon, death, 2,000 years ago. Christians need not fear him. Satan does nothing without God's knowledge. God has ultimate control.

Timothy may verbalize doubts about the kind of God that would allow Satan's presence and power on this earth to cause suffering. Depending upon Timothy's receptivity, you may want to share verses on God's sovereignty as well as His goodness.

Case Study A: Adam and Eve

Read Genesis 3:1-5 together. Work through the following questions:

Q: What is the progression of the temptations? (Eve saw, she took, she ate, then gave to her husband.)

Q: What did she observe about the fruit? (It was good for food, pleasing to the eye, desirable for gaining wisdom.)

Q: What did they do once they realized they were naked? (They covered themselves.)

Q: How did they react when God was walking in the garden? (They were afraid.)

Q: How did God respond? (He asked two questions.)

Q: How did Adam respond? (He blamed others.)

Discuss with Timothy the basic principles regarding temptation that are revealed in this passage: Satan appeals to our senses and casts doubt on God's Word and character. Temptation is a slippery slope toward sin. Adam and Eve see the fruit and take it, giving in to temptation. They sin by eating the fruit, trying to hide what they did, and blaming others for their actions.

Q: Have you seen this progression at work in your life?

Scripture vs. Temptation

The question in the center of page 43 emphasizes the fact that Jesus quoted Scripture every time to refute Satan. Discuss how Jesus might have spent time in Hebrew school memorizing Scripture, hiding it in His heart. Make a point to apply this truth to the importance of Timothy's Scripture memorization efforts.

Spiritual Armor

Make sure Timothy has identified all the various parts of the armor of God as described in the beginning of this lesson (page 37).

Q: Why is it important for you and me to take advantage of the "full armor" of God?

Q: According to this passage, why do we need to?

Page 44:

V. How Do We Have Victory?

Q: Does the image of a "roaring lion" change your view of Satan? How?

★ Emphasize this question from the book.

Q: What is helpful about the knowledge described in verse 9 (1 Peter 5:8-9)?

Note: In verse 8, the word "devour" is literally to "discredit." So Satan is looking for Christians whom he can discredit. "Resist" means "to stand up against." We do this by remaining firm in the Christian faith and in accordance with God's Word. As the believer understands and obeys God's truth, Satan is resisted.

Scouting Report

Be as specific as you can be in your own answers and encourage Timothy to be specific too. For example, "I struggle with lust" is general as opposed to, "I will be traveling out of town this week. The X-rated movies available in the hotel rooms are a big temptation. I will commit to avoid these and choose some healthy activities instead, such as reading a good book, spending some time in the Word and prayer, calling friends in the city who are growing Christians. If I feel overwhelmed with temptation, I will call my Timothy, my wife or friend and share my struggles and ask for prayer."

The Final Score

Discuss some of the statements about how God wins – and so do we. We can take comfort in the fact that Satan has been defeated, found guilty, but in a way is "out on probation" until his final sentencing.

Page 46

Memory Verse: Battling the World, the Flesh and the Devil

Q: How does this Scripture Memory Verse capture the key point of this lesson?

Next Steps

1. Set a day and time to get together again.

2. Encourage your Timothy to consider the Additional Resources, the Optional Applications and listen to the audio for this chapter on CD or at operationtimothy.com and consider watching *The Lion, The Witch and The Wardrobe* with your spouses.

3. Assign Chapter 4, "Dealing with Temptation."

4. Make a note of any questions you could not answer using the Notes section at the end of each chapter.

5. Update your diary and pray for your Timothy this week.

Chapter 4: Dealing with Temptation

The Big Idea: To teach Timothy the basis of a life of obedience and what we are to do if we stray from the path.

Key Teaching Points

- We obey because God loves us, and we love him.

- Everyone will be tempted in this life and everyone will fail.

- When we fail, God has provided a means of forgiveness through Christ. Our relationship with God is not severed, but our fellowship may be. Confession restores our fellowship.

- Ongoing obedience is a process that is made possible through our knowledge of God's Word and His Spirit's enabling; we cannot do it on our own.

Teaching Outline

I. Understanding Temptation
When we sin we lose direction in life.

II. How Can I Find the Path Again?
When we confess our sin, we find the right path again. Confessing to another person and praying with another person is helpful to finding the path.

III. How Do I Stay on the Path?
Through good teaching we know the right path, and, when we stray, rebuking and correction lead us back. However, it is training that will show us how to stay on the path.

IV. The Fruits of Obedience

This lesson picks up the theme of temptation from the previous chapter. Begin by reviewing the Scripture memory verse. This time, you go first.

Page 49:

Crossroads

Q: How is *temptation* simply another word for *choice*?

Page 52:

I. Understanding Temptation

Q: How does temptation make you feel, especially when you give into it?

Page 53:

A Path Out

★ Emphasize this question from the book.

Q: What three assurances regarding temptation are given in 1 Corinthians 10:13?

BK2: 14

Cover each question and work through the Scriptures in this section carefully. The implied message here is that we will fail, and when we fail, we lose direction in life, but we are not lost. We can find the path of obedience once again.

Page 54:

II. How Can I Find the Path Again?

Q: What are the things that you struggle with?

Don't Go It Alone

Timothy will probably name you as one person with whom sharing is possible. If you are the only one, it may indicate that close relationships are a problem. Encourage Timothy to develop friendships, attend church, CBMC team meetings, small group Bible studies, etc.

Page 55:

Q: Look closely, do you see two men in this picture? This is not an example of one man pulling another man down, but of one man coming alongside of another man to help.

Page 56:

III. How Do I Stay on the Path?

 Emphasize this question from the book.

Q: How would you restate this in your own words?

If Timothy does not know how to reword step four in the path, work through it together. But don't get sidetracked. There may be a tendency to spend more time on the first step dealing with God's will at the expense of the second which deals with obedience. There will be an entire study on God's will in *Life Perspectives*.

Use an example from your own life to walk through the four steps in the path. Without taking too much time, illustrate how God used your family, friends, and others as a means of support, rebuke, and correction. Tell how you got back on the path and what you learned in the process.

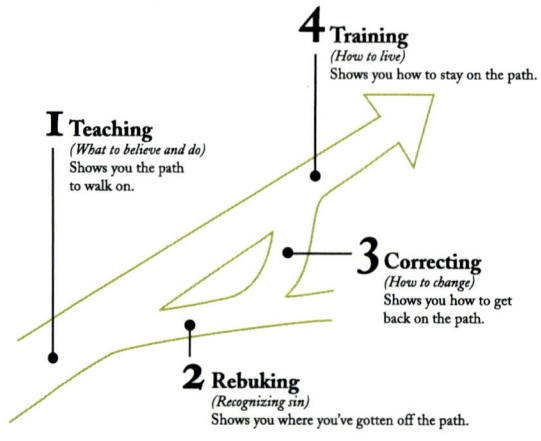

chapter 4 – dealing with temptation

Page 58:

Spend time in Romans 6:12-14 and the surrounding verses.

The Christian life requires *balance*. There is always tension regarding friends and companions. On the one hand, we encourage Timothy to stay in contact with "lost friends" while at the same time we encourage fellowship with "wise" Christians. However, in the Proverbs 13:20 passage, the emphasis is on "wise counsel."

Page 59:

IV. The Fruits of Obedience

After covering the questions on John 14:21, keep reading verses 23-24, then ask:

Q: What comes first: obedience or love? (It is not a matter of either/or, rather it's both.)

Love results in obedience; obedience demonstrates love is genuine.

Q: Is the motivation for obedience a matter of must or will? I must obey, or I will obey? Why?

When the Holy Spirit comes, He gives new willingness and love for God that result in "I will" rather than "I must." Duty and obligation are only good for the short-term, while love and willingness are long-term motivators.

Page 60:

Displacement

Read the section on displacement and focus on how to keep your mind pure in Philippians 4:8.

Summary: Remember the illustration of the railroad tracks? In Rick Warren's *The Purpose Driven Life* on page 202, he talks about the choice and temptation: God develops the fruit of the Spirit in your life by allowing you to experience circumstances in which you're tempted to express the exact opposite quality! Character development always involves a choice, and temptation provides that opportunity.

Page 62:

Memory Verse: Dealing with Temptation

Q: How does this Scripture Memory Verse capture the key point of this lesson?

Q: When tempted, what does 1 Corinthians 10:13 tell us to do?

(Answer: Look for the exit signs.)

Next Steps

1. Set a day and time to get together again.

2. Encourage your Timothy to consider the Additional Resources, the Optional Applications, and listen to the audio for this chapter on CD or at operationtimothy.com. Consider watching *The Mission* as couples.

3. Assign Chapter 5, "Discovering the Holy Spirit."

4. Make a note of any questions you could not answer using the Notes section at the end of each chapter.

5. Update your diary and pray for your Timothy this week.

Notes

> **REMINDER:** Operation Timothy is based on Paul's instruction to young Timothy in 2 Timothy 2:2, "And the things you have heard me say in the presence of many witnesses entrust to reliable men who will also be qualified to teach others."
>
> Suggest to your "Timothy" that he begin praying about a man that he may disciple.

Chapter 5: Discovering the Holy Spirit

The Big Idea: To emphasize the important role of the Holy Spirit in the life of every Christian and to help the Timothy understand exactly who the Holy Spirit is and why He is important in our lives right now.

Key Teaching Points

- The Holy Spirit is God, and He is a very important member of the Trinity – Father, Son, and Holy Spirit.
- Every believer has the indwelling of the Holy Spirit.
- The Holy Spirit is often overlooked, not understood, or underappreciated.
- The Holy Spirit is a valuable resource for each of us. He serves many functions, including linking us to the Father, convicting us of sin, giving us the ability to recognize sin and abstain from it, and giving us the spiritual gifts.
- Living a life yielded to and led by the Holy Spirit is the best way to stay connected to the Father and to produce ample spiritual fruit.

Teaching Outline

I. Who Is The Holy Spirit?
   i. The Holy Spirit is a person.
   ii. He is high power, but low key. He is a helper.

II. Who Has The Holy Spirit?
   He lives in the hearts of believers, not everyone.

III. What Does The Holy Spirit Do?
   i. His Role
   ii. His Gifts

IV. How Does One Live and Work with the Holy Spirit?
   i. Getting our House in Order
   ii. The Fruit of The Holy Spirit

This lesson introduces us to the Holy Spirit, who is a valuable resource as we battle the world, the flesh, and the devil which we discussed in previous chapters. The Holy Spirit is a somewhat mysterious element of the Godhead, but can be a valuable partner for us if we recognize and understand His roles and His capabilities. Begin by asking Timothy to recite the Scripture memory verse and ask him how he feels about this fruit. Is it evident in his life? Would he like it to be?

Page 65:

What's in a Name?

Q: How do you think this picture signifies the Holy Spirit? How would you describe the Holy Spirit? Have you ever experienced the Holy Spirit?

Page 67:

I. Who Is the Holy Spirit?

The Holy Spirit is a person.

Q: Have you always thought of the Holy Spirit as a person? What do you learn from the Genesis or Psalms passages that indicate that the Holy Spirit is really a person?

Cover the two questions and Scriptures carefully. These Scriptures start to lay the groundwork for the important point that we can have a relationship with the Holy Spirit. Here are a few other Scripture verses to refer to if Timothy struggles with these concepts: Matthew 3:16 and 28:19; John 15:26-27; Acts 1:4-5; Romans 8; 1 Corinthians 12:3-6; 2 Corinthians 3:18 and 13:14; Ephesians 4:4-6; 1 Peter 1:2; Jude 20.

Low Key, High Power

Q: How important is the Holy Spirit within the Godhead/Trinity?

The Holy Spirit is obviously very important. Try to help your Timothy discover the many important roles as you go through this chapter and dig into the Scripture verses. Additional verses are: Ephesians 3:14-15; Ephesians 6:18; 2 Peter 1:21; etc.

Three in one illustrations: Emphasize that all earthly or human analogies to the Trinity fall short of completely describing the mystery and the full scope of this truth, but these four illustrations may give the Timothy some better understanding.

Page 68:

Get the Picture

These three symbols may help to begin the process of your Timothy understanding the exciting amorphous or fluid symbolism associated with the Holy Spirit. This may be a good time to ask your Timothy if he has ever seen a fictional movie or read a fictional book where the Holy Spirit was portrayed. The Baggar Vance character in the movie *The Legend of Baggar Vance* is often described as a "Holy Spirit" character.

Q: Do you see any element of the Holy Spirit in the waterfall picture?

II. Who Has the Holy Spirit?

Here to Help

★ Emphasize these questions from the book (page 69).

Q: Read John 7:38-39. For whom is the Spirit available?

Your Heart, a Home for God

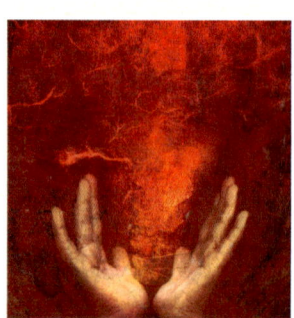

Q: How would/should we know if someone has the Holy Spirit?

Page 70:

Q: What do you think this red picture represents?

Page 71:

Q: What do you think this picture of a man walking with a cane represents in the context of The Holy Spirit?

Q: Who do you look to for guidance and direction?

Page 72:

III. What Does the Holy Spirit Do?

This is an important element of the chapter. Your Timothy should have a good understanding of the roles and responsibilities of the Holy Spirit. In this section, there are three general roles of the Holy Spirit discussed, and of course, there are many specific responsibilities mentioned throughout the Scriptures. Take your time and go through each of these questions so that your Timothy can begin to see the vital role played by the Holy Spirit.

Page 73:

Q. Given all this information about the Holy Spirit, what would you think would be the best way to absorb it and appreciate the Holy Spirit?

Page 74:

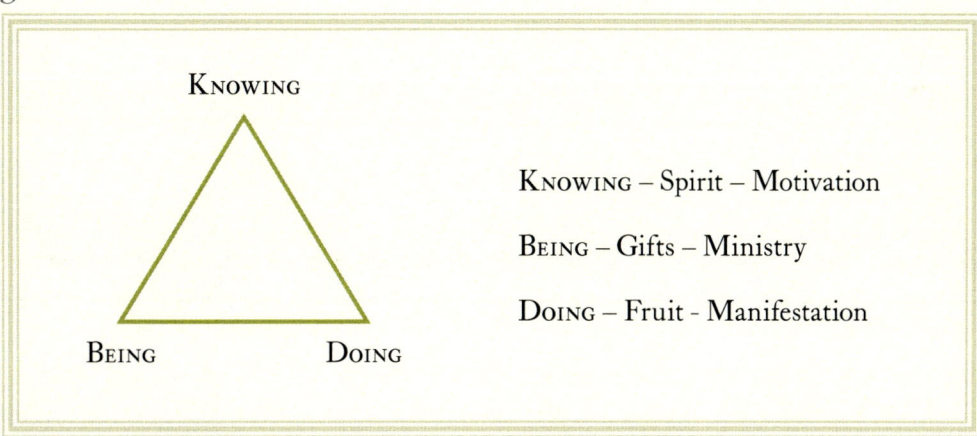

Q: How would you rank your success in these three areas as it applies to the ministry of the Holy Spirit?

Q: Where are you strongest and where do you need to put more focus?

Page 75:

Gifts for Everyone

This can be an interesting discussion. If Timothy has not heard of spiritual gifts or has a background where certain gifts were emphasized to the exclusion of others, you might want to spend some time looking up the Scriptures listed beside each. In addition, if Timothy does not know what his gifts are you might mention that he should be able to search on the internet for "spiritual gifts inventories" (example: http://mintools.com/spiritual-gifts-test.htm) and find some simple on-line assessments to help him determine his giftedness.

Page 76:

Q: Do you sometimes feel that you are asked to perform in areas where you have absolutely no giftedness?

Q: What are your areas of spiritual giftedness?

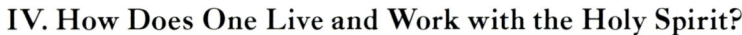

IV. How Does One Live and Work with the Holy Spirit?

Getting Your House in Order

Q. Precisely how will you prepare your heart for the indwelling of the Holy Spirit?

Romans 6:11-14 describes some general suggestions for your "house cleaning," and *My Heart, Christ's Home* by Robert Boyd Munger is an excellent little booklet that compares our hearts to a physical house. It is a good resource for depicting our bodies as homes for the Holy Spirit. It is inexpensive and would make a great gift for your Timothy.

Fresh Fruit in Season

There is an important contrast to be made between acts of a sinful nature (Galatians 5:19-21) and the fruit of the Spirit (Galatians 5:22-23). In today's world we often are directly confronted by the first list and only through the power of the Holy Spirit can we produce the great fruit of verses 22 and 23!

Page 77:

Q. What must we do to produce fresh fruit in our lives?

chapter 5 - discovering the Holy Spirit

Page 78:

Memory Verse: Discovering the Holy Spirit

Q: How does this Scripture Memory Verse capture the key point of this lesson?

Next Steps

1. Set a day and time to get together again.

2. Encourage your Timothy to consider the Additional Resources, the Optional Applications, and listen to the audio for this chapter on CD or at operationtimothy.com. Consider watching *The Legend of Bagger Vance*.

3. Assign Chapter 6, "Communicating With God."

4. Encourage your Timothy to take a spiritual gifts inventory if appropriate.

5. Make a note of any questions you could not answer using the Notes section at the end of each chapter.

6. Update your diary and pray for your Timothy this week.

NOTES

_____
_____
_____
_____
_____
_____
_____
_____
_____
_____
_____

> REMINDER: Operation Timothy is based on Paul's instruction to young Timothy in 2 Timothy 2:2, "And the things you have heard me say in the presence of many witnesses entrust to reliable men who will also be qualified to teach others."
>
> Suggest to your "Timothy" that he begin praying about a man that he may disciple.

Chapter 6: Communicating with God

The Big Idea: To help Timothy learn that prayer is the primary means of communicating with God, highlight its benefits and demonstrate how to develop a more effective prayer life.

Key Teaching Points

- Praying may consist of praise, thanksgiving, confession, and asking for help for oneself and others.

- God answers all prayers – yes, no, or wait; yet there are some conditions for prayer (belief, pure heart, unselfish motives).

- A "Ten Most Wanted" prayer list helps us focus on people we desire to come to Christ.

- A quiet time is a vital and special time alone with God to hear from Him, share our hearts, and be directed by Him.

Teaching Outline

I. What are the Essentials of Prayer?
There are five essentials of prayer: praise, thanksgiving, confession, prayer for others and for ourselves.

II. What Are the Benefits of Prayer?
Prayer relieves our anxiety and stress and allows us to live a life of inward peace.

III. For Whom Do I Pray?
We are instructed to pray especially for the unsaved, for more workers to share their faith, for authorities, and for those who mistreat us.

IV. How Do We Spend Time with God?
We are to spend a quiet time alone with God, for adoration, confession, thanksgiving, and supplication.

Page 81:

Q: What does this picture make you think of?

Page 83:

I. What are the Essentials of Prayer?

Q: What is the difference between confident praying and presumptuous praying? How can we come to God in confidence and humility at the same time?

Share your disappointing answers to prayer and what you have learned as a result.

chapter 6 - communicating with God

A couple of wise thoughts on prayer:

"Much of our difficulty as seeking Christians stems from our unwillingness to take God as He is and adjust our lives accordingly. We insist upon trying to modify Him and to bring Him nearer our own image. The flesh whimpers against the inexorable sentence and begs like Agag for a little mercy, a little indulgence of its carnal ways. It is no use. We can get a right start only by accepting God as He is and learning to love Him for what He is. As we go on to know Him better, we shall find it a source of unspeakable joy that God is just what He is. Some of the most rapturous moments we know will be those we spend in reverent admiration of the Godhead. In those holy moments the very thought of change in Him will be too painful to endure."

– A. W. Tozer, *The Pursuit of God*

"What is prayer? Prayer is not so much an act as it is an attitude – an attitude of dependency, dependency upon God. Prayer is a confession of creature weakness, yea, of helplessness. Prayer is the acknowledgment of our need and the spreading of it before God. We do not say that this is all there is in prayer; it is not. But it is the essential, the primary element in prayer...Therefore, prayer is the very opposite of dictating to God. Because prayer is an attitude of dependency, the one who really prays is submissive, submissive to the Divine will; and submission to the Divine will means that we are content for the Lord to supply our need according to the dictates of His own sovereign pleasure. And hence it is that we say, every prayer that is offered to God in this spirit is sure of meeting with an answer or response from Him."

– A. W. Pink, *The Sovereignty of God*

Page 86:

Q: What is your reaction to 'praying without ceasing'?

Page 87:

The Perfect Script

At first, we were unsure about how to pray, but He helps us. The Holy Spirit knows us and His own will better than we ever will, and He is praying for us as well as praying with us (Romans 8).

Discuss various phrases in the Lord's Prayer. For example, what does it mean to ask God to forgive our debts/trespasses in the same way we forgive others?

Q: Do you really want God to forgive you the same way you forgive others?

BK2: 24

Page 89:

II. What Are the Benefits of Prayer?

Q: Is there one area of your life about which you would like to experience this peace? If so, share it.

Martin Luther said, "Prayer is not overcoming God's reluctance, but laying hold of His willingness."

Page 91:

III. For Whom Do I Pray?

Paul's eloquent prayer in Ephesians 3:14-21 can be applied to people on your prayer list. In fact, praying Scripture back to God is a wonderful way to communicate with God. If Timothy prayed through these verses for someone, suggest that he write a note telling them so.

Page 92:

Take time to discuss and pray for the people you have on your lists. Encourage Timothy to use the CBMC Ten Most Wanted Card. This is also a good time to ask him who he is going to take through *Operation Timothy*.

Page 93:

Too Busy Not to Pray

"We are too busy to pray, and so we are too busy to have power. We have a great deal of activity, but we accomplish little; many services but few conversions; much machinery but few results."
– R. A. Torrey, (1856-1928) an American evangelist, pastor, educator, and author.

IV. How Do We Spend Time with God?

Cover this section thoroughly. Share your personal ups and downs, as well as practical tips regarding your quiet time (time, place, what you do, etc.); encourage Timothy to find a plan that works. In addition to the practical suggestions in the book, here are a few more.

1. The book notes the Bibles formatted for reading in one year. There are also many Bible reading plans available online or through a church (maybe a Christian bookstore). You could give him a pamphlet with a plan for reading His current Bible instead of recommending he purchase another Bible.

2. Bible reading plans are also available through email and RSS feeds. If Timothy would prefer to read the Bible on his computer or phone, you could help him find a reading plan on the Internet.

3. Precept Ministries has many Bible studies from simple to involved, most of which teach study principles that can help Timothy make strong observations during his Bible reading.

4. Another recommendation for reading the Bible is to read one book several times and make a few notes before moving on to the next one. You could also read five chapters of the book every day for a month before going to the next five chapters. In this way, you can get to know that part of Scripture very well.

Q: Do you currently have a plan for spending time with God? (Help Timothy to be realistic about beginning or continuing a time with God).

Page 96:

Memory Verse: Communicating with God

Q: How does this Scripture Memory Verse capture the key point of this lesson?

Next Steps

1. Make sure Timothy has a "Ten Most Wanted" Card.

2. Set a day and time to get together again.

3. Encourage Timothy to consider the Additional Resources, the Optional Applications, and listen to the audio for this chapter on CD or at operationtimothy.com.

4. Assign Chapter 7, "Telling Others Our Story."

5. Make a note of any questions you could not answer using the Notes section at the end of each chapter.

6. Pray for Timothy this week and update diary.

Chapter 7: Telling Others Our Story

The Big Idea: To become more effective as a witness for Christ, we will clarify our message (the hope of Christ) and how we came to know Him – with specific help enabling Timothy to write out that unique story.

Key Teaching Points

- God has called all believers to share their faith – there are no exceptions.
- The message is clear and simple: Christ, as God, became a man who lived, died and rose again to forgive our sins. Only as we receive this gift of a relationship with Christ will we experience forgiveness and have eternal life.
- Every Christian has a story to tell: his life without Christ, how he came to know Him personally, his changed and changing life with Christ.

Teaching Outline

I. What Is My Testimony?
My testimony is the factual account of how God has changed my life.

II. Why Should I Tell Others?
Although some may be hesitant to do so at first, Jesus has commanded us to share our faith.

III. What Should I Say?
Our message is simple, and the Holy Spirit will provide the words.

IV. Who Should I Tell?
We are to share the gospel with those in our sphere of influence to the level they are ready to receive it.

This is a lengthy lesson. Take as many weeks as you need to work through completely. Begin with a review of the current memory verse, then work through the previous verses.

Page 99:

While we will never be as famous as Jerry Seinfeld, we all have a story.

Read through Acts 26 together, making note of key principles that surface in the passage.

I. What is My Testimony?

Don't be surprised if Timothy has not completed this section. This is a long session. Simply work through any unfinished portions, discussing and filling in the appropriate blanks as you do. You can refine the material later – just get it down now.

You many notice some reluctance on Timothy's part. Satan would love to cause confusion and bring up doubts.

chapter 7 - telling others our story

If Timothy has completed the testimony section, have him read it aloud to you. Repeat back some of the essential points and give plenty of praise. Share what made an impact on you as you listened. Have Timothy spend some time next week polishing it.

Be sensitive. As Timothy works on his testimony, he may see that his life has not changed. Timothy may think he is a Christian, but is not, and he may or may not see his need to submit to Christ now. If so, review *Life Questions* (Book 1), lesson 6 with him.

Be aware that your Timothy may not have a life story that fits the outline we follow in this chapter. He may have been saved at an early age and is only now being discipled. So, he may not have anything to say about his past life or the circumstances of his conversion. If Timothy is a genuine believer, he will have wrestled with sins (big or small from our perspective) and seen the fruit of the Spirit in his life. His testimony can point to the Lord's faithfulness or to the emptiness of religious life and the struggle of obeying the Lord in one's own strength and out of personal pride. Help him see how God has worked in him and through him over the years.

Page 102:

Q: Why do you think having possible introductions to your testimony would be valuable?

Page 104:

Q: What was the most striking change in your life after you became a Christian?

Page 106:

Q: What is the primary motivation for our story?

Page 107:

★ Emphasize this question from the book.

Q: How did you learn or hear about how to become a Christian?

Page 111:

II. Why Should I Tell Others?

Q: What seems to be getting in the way as you attempt to share your faith with others? Discuss problems you are facing personally in this area.

Q: The best offense is a good defense! Why do you think being ready to give our story is so important?

BK2: 28

Page 112:

III. What Should I Say?

Effective Communication

Discuss the importance gentleness and respect play in effective communication. Give examples of how we can come across in a condescending or harsh manner, if we are not careful.

Read through Acts 1:8, John 3:16, and 1 Corinthians 15:1-6, underscoring the essential points. This lesson assumes that Timothy is or has become a Christian. However, many people have stated that it was only when they started to write out their testimony that they fully understood the gospel and accepted Christ. Be sensitive to this fact.

Page 114:

IV. Who Should I Tell?

1. Raising the Flag

Brainstorm together and jot down as many one-sentence flag-raisers as you can in five minutes. Record them in the Notes section on page 116 and 118.

When we share our faith, we are as a lighthouse to those who are lost.

Page 115:

2. Faith Stories

Work through events in your lives that would classify as "faith stories," and take time to write one out on page 118. Use an outline form, do not include details.

Discuss the testimony diagram and point out the progression, noting how the sharing tools fit with the cultivation process.

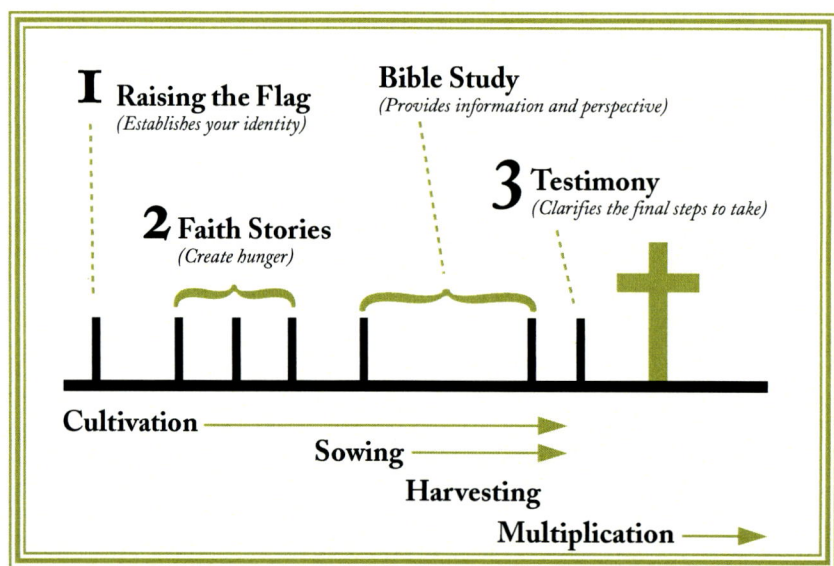

chapter 7 - telling others our story

Living Proof

Encourage Timothy to pray about going through a *Living Proof* video study group. You, as a leader, might consider starting one, inviting Timothy and your spouses to join you, along with several other couples.

The *Living Proof* drama is gripping and relates to the common struggles with which we all deal in growing and sharing our faith with others. The series is designed to be flexible, allowing you to meet once a week, twice a month or even once a month. It can be used in a Sunday School format, taking two sessions per Sunday.

Note: *Living Proof* is available through cbmc.com.

Page 116:

Memory Verse: Telling Others Our Story

Q: How does this Scripture Memory Verse capture the key point of this lesson?

Next Steps

I. Refer to the "Ten Most Wanted" card. (Give him a card if he does not have one). Inquire about the people on the list, who they are, how long a relationship has existed, what concerns there may be.

II. Encourage your Timothy to consider the Additional Resources, the Optional Applications, and listen to the audio for this chapter on CD or at operationtimothy.com.

III. Give Timothy *Life Perspectives* and assign Chapter 1, "Digging into the Bible." Go over the table of contents, highlighting what you will learn together.

IV. Set a day and time to get together again.

V. Make a note of any questions you could not answer using the Notes section at the end of each chapter.

VI. Pray for your Timothy this week and update diary.

REMINDER: Operation Timothy is based on Paul's instruction to young Timothy in 2 Timothy 2:2, "And the things you have heard me say in the presence of many witnesses entrust to reliable men who will also be qualified to teach others."

Suggest to your "Timothy" that he begin praying about a man that he may disciple.

leader's guide for book 3

LIFE PERSPECTIVES
SUGGESTED DISCUSSIONS AND QUESTIONS

Chapter 1: Digging Into the Bible

The Big Idea: To assist Timothy in gaining a greater understanding of the purpose of the Bible, what it means on a personal level and how to begin to study it on his own.

Key Teaching Points

- The Bible is God's message to man on who He is, what His promises to us are, and how we are to live.

- In order to gain a deeper understanding of the Bible, we need to have a balance of hearing, reading, studying, memorizing, and meditating upon the Scriptures.

- When studying or meditating on a passage, it helps to ask the questions: What? So what? Now what?

Teaching Outline

I. What Is the Purpose of the Bible?
   The Bible exists to teach, rebuke, correct, and train us.

II. How Does the Bible Help Me?
   The Bible reveals God's character and activity in the world. It shows us the good news of Christ's redeeming work and points us to Christ Jesus on every page. It instructs and illustrates how we are to live the Christian life.

III. What Will I Do with the Bible?
   The Bible will help train us how to live only if we apply what it says.

Page 1:

That's What They Say

Q: What is your reaction to these quotes?

Take time to understand how your Timothy's view of the Bible has changed since *Life Questions*, chapter 2, "Is the Bible Credible?"

Q: How does our culture view the Bible? A relic? Myths? Stories?

Q: As you consider the Bible's impact on your life, what are your thoughts?

Page 3:

I. What Is the Purpose of the Bible?

Q: As an answer to the question on the purpose of the Bible, what do you think of the last sentence in the first paragraph on page 3, "Because our very ability to know and understand God is found in them"?

Page 4:

Q: What is your reaction to the caption, "Our faith in Christ hinges on our faith in these written words"?

Page 5:

Q: What would happen if 40 people from many countries and various languages wrote a book, with each individual taking a chapter? Would it make sense?

II. How Does the Bible Help Me?

Answers for the chart on Psalm 19:7-11

Verse	Bible is Called	Characteristics	What is does for me
7	Law	Perfect	Refreshes me spiritually
7	Statues	Trustworthy	Gives me wisdom
8	Commands	Right	Brings joy to my heart
8	Commands	Dear	Giving insight to life
9	Laws	True	Each is fair for me
10		More precious than gold, sweeter than honey	
11		Warning	Warns me. Great reward for those who obey

If your Timothy had difficulty with the chart on Psalms 19, work through it together. Some of the attitudes and actions are interchangeable; the main emphasis is the content of the verses, not filling in the chart correctly.

Page 7:

Digging for Treasure

	Attitude	Action
9	Desire purity	Living by His Word
10	Seeking God with all your heart	Prayer for faithfulness
11	Desire to not sin against God	Hidden His Word in my heart
12	Desire to be taught	Teach Statutes

13	Willingness to tell others	Tell of Your judgments/laws
14	Rejoice	Rejoice in following Your statutes/decrees
15	Consider Your way	Meditate on the precepts
16	Delight in Decrees	Will not neglect Your Word

Hidden in a Safe Place (A case for memorizing Scripture)

As a disciple, Timothy must know and use God's Word, to be victorious over sin.

> "How can a young man keep his way pure? By living according to your word... I have hidden your word in my heart that I might not sin against you" (Psalm 119:9, 11).

When temptations come along, you can call up a verse from memory that specifically addresses the temptation.

> "These commandments that I give you today are to be upon your hearts" (Deuteronomy 6:6).

God instructed the Jews to have His Words in their hearts. See Deuteronomy 11:18-21. The same principle is also beneficial to Christians.

> "Let the word of Christ dwell in you richly as you teach and admonish one another with all wisdom, and as you sing psalms, hymns and spiritual songs with gratitude in your hearts to God" (Colossians 3:16).

Having God's Word memorized makes you a more effective witness for Him. God can use you, and the verses you have memorized, to bring others to Him. Remember, you may not always have a Bible handy when you need it.

> "But in your hearts set apart Christ as Lord. Always be prepared to give an answer to everyone who asks you to give the reason for the hope that you have. But do this with gentleness and respect" (1 Peter 3:15).

Dr. Chuck Swindoll has written:

> "I know of no other single practice in the Christian life more rewarding, practically speaking, than memorizing Scripture...No other single exercise pays greater spiritual dividends! Your prayer life will be strengthened. Your witnessing will be sharper and much more effective. Your attitudes and outlook will begin to change. Your mind will become alert and observant. Your confidence and assurance will be enhanced. Your faith will be solidified" (from *Growing Strong in the Seasons of Life*).

Page 8:

Q: In 1 John 2:5 (NLT), it says, "But those who obey God's word really do love him. That is the way to know whether or not we live in him." What is the connection between loving God and His Word?

Page 9:

Q: Have you ever meditated?

While there may be some negative connotations to meditation, especially if Timothy was involved in activities such as transcendental meditation, let him know that meditating on God's Word is healthy. You may want to share with him the definition of *meditate* from Webster's 1828 Dictionary:

"To dwell on anything in thought; to contemplate; to study; to turn or revolve any subject in the mind; appropriately but not exclusively used of pious contemplation, or a consideration of the great truths of religion. 'His delight is in the law of the Lord, and in his law doth he meditate day and night' (Psalm 1)."

Page 10:

Get a grip. Here's a "hands on" approach to living and working with the Word of God.

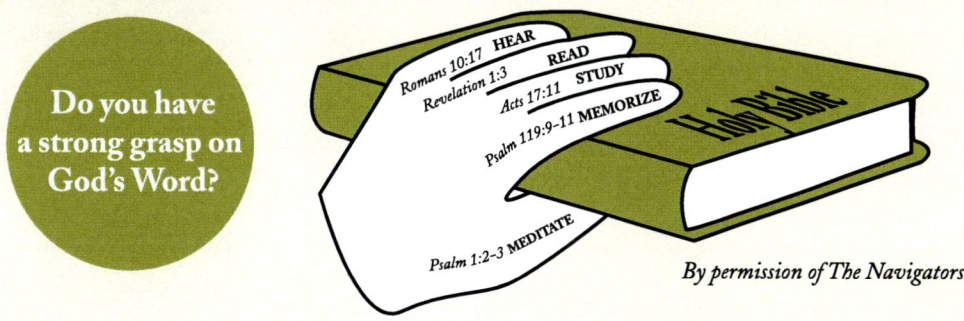

By permission of The Navigators

The Hand: An Illustration

Pick up the Bible with one hand. Transfer it over to the other hand, but try to hold it only by your little finger. It will naturally fall. Try again, this time holding it with the little finger and the thumb only. It can be grasped in this way, but can be easily pulled out of your grasp. (Have Timothy take the Bible out of your hand.) Then, demonstrate the increasing grip you have physically on the Bible as you add each finger along with the thumb. When all five fingers are gripping the Bible, Timothy will have a difficult time getting it out of your grasp. This visually demonstrates the spiritual principle of getting a strong grip on God's Word. It takes not just one or two of these means, but all five to ensure a sturdy grasp of God's Word. Meditation is the key to each of the other four.

III. What will I do with the Bible?

The three questions (see below) provide a simple yet effective method of studying a passage of scripture or a complete chapter. Spend some time on how a method like this, with the guidance of the Holy Spirit, is crucial to growing in Christ.

1. What?	2. So What?	3. Now What?
Observation	*Personalization*	*Application*
What does it say?	What does it say to me?	What will I do?
v.1 Man is blessed by not walking, standing, sitting with evil or evil-doers.	I need to choose carefully whom I will follow and spend time with and where I go.	I'll examine who I'm following and where I spend time to see if the influence is good or evil.
v.2		

Page 11:

★ Emphasize this question from the book.

Q: (Note the picture of the tree on page 12) How is the Christian like a tree?

Discuss how the picture shows the top half of the tree, but the unseen roots are strong and go down deep. This is a metaphor for life. Explain that everyone wants beautiful fruit in their lives and may tend to focus on the "top half" of their life, the part that can be seen. It takes strong roots in God's Word to provide the nourishment necessary for growth.

Page 14:

Studying, meditating and applying God's Word every day—for the Christian it's as necessary and instinctive as breathing.

Memory Verse: Digging Into the Bible

Q: "How does this Scripture Memory Verse capture the key point of this lesson?"

Next Steps

1. Set a day and time to get together again.

2. Encourage your Timothy to consider the Additional Resources and the Optional Applications. For example: Listen to the CD or download the message from operationtimothy.com for Chapter 1 of *Life Perspectives*.

3. Assign Chapter 2, "Knowing God's Will."

4. Make a note of any questions you could not answer using the Notes section at the end of each chapter.

5. Update your diary and pray for your Timothy this week.

Chapter 2: Knowing God's Will

The Big Idea: To understand that God has a plan and purpose for each of us. It is not a matter of having God rubber stamp our plan, rather, a matter of participating in His purposes.

Key Teaching Points

- God has a plan and purpose for every one of His children. He has a universal purpose which includes everyone: to love Him, worship Him, be a witness for Him, to be thankful, abstain from immorality, etc.

- His unique will for us begins as we surrender our will and desires and fully follow Christ.

- God is interested in our hearts and how we proceed as He is in what we do.

- A right relationship with God is essential to hearing God's direction for us moment by moment.

Teaching Outline

I. Does God have a Plan?
God has an intimate plan for you and an ultimate plan for the world.

II. Knowing God's will for everyone
The Bible contains the essence of God's will for mankind.

III. Discerning God's will
Through prayer, the study of the Word, and wise counsel we can discern God's will for us.

IV. Keeping the Channels Clear
Sin and lack of accountability can bring confusion to direction in life.

Page 17:

The Greatest Question

Q: Did you get the brain teaser (at the bottom/left side of the page)?

If not, it may be fun to go to the end of the chapter and read the answer to the brain teaser.

Q: If you could directly ask God one question, what would it be?

Chances are, it would relate to His will for your future, possibly in the area of vocation or other major life decision.

Page 19:

I. Does God Have a Plan?

★ Emphasize these questions from the book.

Q: Read Ephesians 1:10-11. Summarize the relationship between God and history described here.

Q: What place do people play in God's scheme, according to this passage?

(Consider reading Ephesians 1:1-11 together and underlining the "we's" and "us's".)

Page 20:

II. God's Will for Everyone

After discussing all the questions, ask Timothy which of the "it is always God's will for you…" statements are difficult for him/her to obey; which ones are being obeyed, disobeyed?

Discuss the J. I. Packer quote from *Knowing God* on page 20.

Page 22:

III. God's Will for You

Q: Have you ever asked God to guide you in an area of life? Did it seem like you heard from Him?

Page 23:

Q: As you wrote out your own version of David's prayer, was there a question you asked God?

Page 24:

CORRECTION to Paul Little quote: Here is a fuller quotation from Paul Little's *Affirming the Will of God* (pg 9):

> "The will of God is dynamic and not static! By recognizing the two aspects of God's will—what is specifically revealed in his Word and what is not—we get away from the static blueprint concept. The will of God is not like a magic package let down out of heaven by a string, a package we must grope after in desperation, hoping to somehow clasp it to our hearts.
>
> "Instead the will of God is like a scroll that unrolls every day. In other words, God will guide you and me today and tomorrow and the next day and the day after that. One day at a time. And he may show us new applications of his commands, which we have previously not noticed.
>
> "Our call, then, is to follow the Lord Jesus Christ, to walk with him in a daily close relationship. It is first of all being, not doing. How you spend your life is more important than where. Neither rules nor a blueprint, neither a specific place nor a particular kind of work comes before our call to follow him. As we realize this, we will begin to sense the exhilaration each day can hold when we are living hand in hand with God—the Holy Spirit guiding us, unrolling the scroll."

(NOTE: Early printings of *Operation Timothy* misquoted part of this passage.)

Page 25:

Read through the section on the bottom half of this page about George Mueller. Use specifics from your own life to discuss these principles.

Q: What significance do these principles have for you?

Page 26:

★ Emphasize this question from the book.

Q: What is your reaction to George Mueller's approach to God's voice?

Page 27:

IV. Keeping the Channels Clear

Read the paragraph at the top of page 27 and underscore the three ways we understand how God guides us.

1. We study God's Word.
2. We pray and seek the leadership of the Spirit.
3. We seek the advice of wise Christians.

Page 28:

Preventative Maintenance

If Timothy has not answered this section, ask questions to discern a particular decision he may be facing at this point. Don't give into the temptation to "tell" Timothy what God's will is for him. Keep asking questions that will allow Timothy to discover how God is leading.

Page 29:

Discuss the response Timothy has written in answer to the question on his current significant decisions.

Memory Verse: Knowing God's Will

Q: How does this Scripture Memory Verse capture the key point of this lesson?

Next Steps

1. Set a day and time to get together again.

2. Encourage your Timothy to consider the Additional Resources, the Optional Applications, and listen to the audio for this chapter on CD or at operationtimothy.com.

3. Assign Chapter 3, "Becoming A Person of Character."

4. Make a note of any questions you could not answer using the Notes section at the end of each chapter.

5. Update your diary and pray for your Timothy this week.

NOTES

> **REMINDER:** Operation Timothy is based on Paul's instruction to young Timothy in 2 Timothy 2:2, "And the things you have heard me say in the presence of many witnesses entrust to reliable men who will also be qualified to teach others."
>
> Suggest to your "Timothy" that he begin praying about a man that he may disciple.

Chapter 3: Becoming a Person of Character

The Big Idea: To understand that God wants us to become people with deep character. Who we are on the inside drives our behavior.

Key Teaching Points

- Developing character is a moral struggle that doesn't begin with us, but begins with Christ in us.

- Character is forged in the fiery furnace of trials and difficulties.

- Humility is the ultimate expression of character, through which God can have free reign in our lives.

- Character begins with my view of God, is reflected in my values, and displayed in my behavior. It is a process that happens from the inside out; changing my behavior doesn't always change my view of God.

Teaching Outline

I. What is character?
Biblical character is defined as inward moral or ethical strength.

II. Why does God develop character?
God's desire is to see us transformed into the likeness of Christ.

III. How God develops character
God uses trials and difficulties to develop our character.

IV. My role in developing character
We are to build our lives on God's view of the world, adhere to values consistent with it, and behave in a manner that reflects the two.

Page 33:

That's What They Say

★ Emphasize these questions from the book:

Q: Which of these quotes strikes you as truth? What do you think the person(s) was trying to communicate?

Q: What is your reaction to the fact that although we are a work in progress (as Christians), that fact should not be used as an excuse to continue to exhibit moral failures?

I. What is Character?

Galatians lists the fruit of the Spirit ("character qualities the Holy Spirit has imparted to us.") They are the evidence that He indwells us – not that we will see any one of these lived out to perfection in our lives. The difference between the work of the Holy Spirit in our lives and the "acts of the sinful nature" are obvious and diametrically opposed.

Read Galatians 5:16-21 with Timothy to compare and contrast the sinful nature's character qualities with those of the Spirit.

Q: How does verse 24 in this passage say we deal with the sinful nature? How do we do this practically?

Character Qualities

- Matthew 7:12   *Respectful, considerate*
- Matthew 5:8   *Purity*
- Romans 13:8   *Pay all debts, love each other*
- 1 Corinthians 15:58   *Perseverance, endurance*
- Colossians 3:13   *Forbearance, forgiving spirit*
- 1 Thessalonians 5:8   *Gratefulness, thankful spirit*
- James 2:8   *Love others as yourself*
- 1 Peter 5:5   *Humble, submissive*

Page 36:

Q: In what ways have you used deception to get what you want?

Page 37:

Q: What does 2 Peter 1:3-9 say about the process of character development? What does verse 8 say in particular? Is there a time factor involved? Does this encourage you/discourage you?

Page 39:

II. Why God Develops Character

★ Emphasize this question from the book.

Q: How does Romans 12:1-2 describe the process of building character?

Note: "Be Transformed" in the Greek is metamorphoo. You might recognize the root of the word metamorphosis.

THE BUTTERFLY: AN ILLUSTRATION

There is a story of a young boy who came upon a cocoon from which a butterfly was struggling to free itself. The boy took pity on the agony of the butterfly's struggle and tried to help by cutting away the cocoon with a pair of scissors, not knowing that the struggle itself is designed to strengthen the wings and enable the butterfly to take flight. The butterfly emerged crippled and unable to fly.

If we are not careful, our efforts to shorten the struggles and lessen our pain or others' pain will cut short the process of our transformation into the likeness of Christ.

Q: In what stage of development are you presently?

chapter 3 – becoming a person of character

Page 40:

III. How God Develops Character

Q: Did you know the story of Tony Dungy's son? Normally, we only hear that he won a Super Bowl. What do you think of how Tony and his wife handled the pain of losing a son?

Page 41:

The Seven Elements of Spiritual Transformation

The illustration is explained in detail in Jim Petersen's book *Lifestyle Discipleship*, Chapter 8. Reading this chapter will give you insight into this lesson. In addition, *Living Proof: Discipleship*, Session 7, vividly portrays this process and explains it in greater detail.

Page 42:

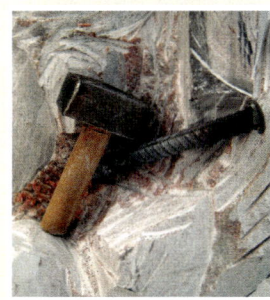

The Visionary Sculptor

Q: How do challenges, suffering, and pain 'sculpt us' into the new creatures He wants us to be?

"Whatever gets dumped into our lives, whatever the source, whether it is bitter or sweet, God can make artful use of it as He makes us over to look like his Son." – Jim Petersen, *Lifestyle Discipleship*

Page 43:

★ Emphasize this question from the book.

Q: What advice can we take from James 5:10-11 to be encouraged in suffering?

Past and Present Pain

Listen carefully and ask questions as Timothy shares.

Timothy may have difficulty with Romans 8:28 and Hebrews 12:7-11, if he was abused as a child or had other deeply painful experiences. Be gentle. Don't attempt to heal a deep wound with a Band-Aid or a pat answer. Listen. Share that our Heavenly Father never abuses us.

IV. My Role in Developing Character

Page 47:

Q: Which has more to do with developing character: worldview or behavior? Why?

The diagram to the right may be helpful in addressing this question.

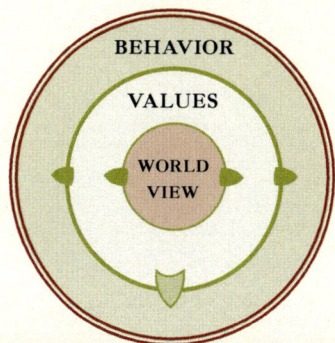

BK3: 12

Page 50:

Memory Verse: Becoming a Person of Character

Q: How does this Scripture Memory Verse capture the key point of this lesson?

Q: What is your reaction to the Summary on page 50 [God is working in and through us to conform and transform us into the living image of Jesus Christ]?

Next Steps

1. Set a day and time to get together again.

2. Encourage your Timothy to consider the Additional Resources, the Optional Applications, and listen to the audio for this chapter on CD or at operationtimothy.com.

3. Assign Chapter 4, "Relationships."

4. Make a note of any questions you could not answer using the Notes section at the end of each chapter.

5. Update your diary and pray for your Timothy this week.

NOTES

REMINDER: Operation Timothy is based on Paul's instruction to young Timothy in 2 Timothy 2:2, "And the things you have heard me say in the presence of many witnesses entrust to reliable men who will also be qualified to teach others."

Suggest to your "Timothy" that he begin praying about a man that he may disciple.

Chapter 4: Relationships

The Big Idea: To cause Timothy to examine relationships with others, including marriage, and to align attitudes and actions with Biblical principles.

Key Teaching Points

- Relationships are part of living the Christian life. They reflect the practical side of our spiritual walk, which is being played out in friendships, associations, marriage, and family.

- God designed marriage in consistency with His nature. Due to sin, there are going to be difficulties, but He has provided instruction in Scripture and His Spirit to help us have good marriages.

Teaching Outline

I. Relationships

  i. Created in the image of God, our desire for relationships reflects the relational nature of God Himself.

  ii. God desires that we grow in fellowship and intimacy with Him. He initiates this by using circumstances, struggles, and trials to reveal Himself and His character.

  iii. A key to understanding relationships is that we all have needs, and these needs should be met within the Body of Christ.

II. Husband – Wife

  i. The Bible has a lot to say about marriage –oneness in spirit, soul, and body.

  ii. Loneliness was replaced by companionship and completion - central to God's design for marriage.

  iii. Husbands are to live with their wives in understanding, and spouses are to meet each other's needs.

  iv. We cannot look to our spouse to establish our personal worth. We must look to Christ.

  v. The best thing we can do for our spouse is to love Jesus more, allowing us to love our partner more completely.

Page 53:

That's What They Say

Q: Do you agree with the statement in the paragraph below this picture, "Relationships are key to life, especially in living the Christian life"? Why or why not?

NOTE: *The quote by Oprah Winfrey in the original version has been replaced with the following:*

"Friendship, true friendship, always lifts. It never drags. Oh, it can be heavy, but it is not destructive. Friendship leads you out of the woods and into the sunlit meadow." – Stu Weber, *Locking Arms*

Page 59:

Read Ephesians 5:21-33 aloud. Discuss the questions about needs and dig into this passage. You may want to look at Philippians 2:1-11 to see how Christ loved the church. Discuss other ways Christ demonstrated His love for the church and gave Himself for her.

Q: What do their expressions in this picture say about this couple's relationship? Does this represent your relationship with your spouse?

Page 60:

★ Emphasize this question from the book.

Q: Comment on the differences between you and your spouse. What difficulties have been caused by these differences?

Page 61:

"Weaker Vessel"– the word in 1 Peter 3:7 referring to the wife as the "weaker vessel" alludes to physical strength, in the sense that most men are physically stronger than their wives. She is equal in Christ and not inferior spiritually because she is a woman, but she does need protection, provision, and strength from her husband.

Q: It is so easy to have a disagreement with our wives. How many of those disagreements would melt away, if we obeyed 1 Peter 3:7 and lived "in an understanding way" with our wives and "granted her honor as a fellow heir of the grace of life?"

Q: In what way does this picture resemble your marriage?

Page 63:

Top Ten Needs

The following Scriptures refer to these needs: Acceptance, *Romans 15:7*; Affection, *Romans 16:16*; Appreciation, *1 Corinthians 11:2*; Approval, *Romans 14:18*; Attention (Care), *1 Corinthians 12:25*; Comfort (Empathy), *1 Thessalonians 4:18*; Encouragement, *1 Thessalonians 5:11*, *Hebrews 10:24*; Respect, *Romans 12:10*; Security, *Mark 9:50*; Support, *Galatians 6:2*.

★ Emphasize this question from the book.

Q: Do you find it difficult to pray with your spouse? Why or why not?

Page 64:

Summary: The Husband-Wife Relationship

Q: Does your relationship with your spouse look like this? In light of this lesson, what can you do to "thaw it out" and have a loving, warm marriage? (Take to heart some of the points made in the summary.)

Memory Verse: Relationships

Q: "How does this Scripture Memory Verse capture the key point of this lesson?"

Next Steps

1. Set a day and time to get together again.

2. Encourage your Timothy to consider the Additional Resources, the Optional Applications, and listen to the audio for this chapter on CD or at operationtimothy.com.

3. Assign Chapter 5, "Kingdom Perspectives."

4. Make a note of any questions you could not answer using the Notes section at the end of each chapter.

5. Update your diary and pray for your Timothy this week.

Notes

Chapter 5: Kingdom Perspectives

The Big Idea: To allow Timothy to understand the Kingdom of God and His view of success, the church and resources.

Key Teaching Points

- How can we understand God's value system versus the value system of the world?
- God does not want us to be "Lone Rangers," but rather involved with others in the fellowship of the church.
- What is the Biblical meaning of success?
- Communicate the difference between ownership and stewardship since everything belongs to God and not us.
- God owns it all and wants us to be faithful stewards of what He has given us.
- Our giving reveals much about our heart attitude toward money and toward God.

Teaching Outline

I. Kingdom Thinking
   i. God is in charge. He is at work around us. We are to align with Him.
   ii. God's view of success, value, purpose, and position is different from the world's perspective.

II. The Church and how do I relate?
   i. The Greek word for "church" in the New Testament refers to all believers who make up the Body of Christ.
   ii. The church is a place for fellowship and to take the message of Christ to the world.
   iii. We thrive in the church as a result of maintaining sound doctrine, using our spiritual gifts to build the Body, and being faithful to Christ.

III. Prosperity and Success
   Help Timothy understand that God's view of prosperity and success is different from the world's.

IV. Stewardship
   Help Timothy understands that God owns everything, and we are to be faithful stewards.

Page 67:

That's What They Say

Q: In light of these statements and your study of *Operation Timothy*, what has changed in your life?

Q: How are we "blinded" by what the world has to offer?

Page 69:

The References column provides the scriptural support in the contrast between worldly thinking versus Kingdom thinking:

	Worldly or Religious Thinking	**Kingdom Thinking (Christ-based Christianity)**	**References**
Pleasure	The goal in life is enjoyment and pleasure. Eat, drink and be merry, you only go around once in life.	Living for God is the source of joy and our joy is made complete in Him.	Luke 9:24 – "For whoever wants to save his life will lose it, but whoever loses his life for me will save it." John 15:11 – "I have told you this so that my joy may be in you and that your joy may be complete."
Recognition and approval	Attaining recognition and approval of people is important. We must have proper self-esteem. We must be acknowledged for our accomplishments.	Seeking God's approval is what really matters and serving others is more valuable than being served.	Romans 14:17-18 – "For the kingdom of God is not a matter of eating and drinking, but of righteousness, peace and joy in the Holy Spirit, because anyone who serves Christ in this way is pleasing to God and approved by men."
Popularity	It's all about whom you know and who knows you.	We are to be servants.	Galatians 1:10 – "Am I now trying to win the approval of men, or of God? Or am I trying to please men? If I were still trying to please men, I would not be a servant of Christ."
Wealth and Status	You deserve the best. Your financial status determines your value as a person. Your position is who you are.	In God's plan our rewards come at the end of this life, based on how we have lived for God, a wealth which does not perish.	Luke 16:15 – "He said to them, "You are the ones who justify yourselves in the eyes of men, but God knows your hearts. What is highly valued among men is detestable in God's sight."

Power	Position and control is the sign of our success.	Be humble and submit yourselves one to another.	1 Peter 5:6-7 – "Humble yourselves, therefore, under God's mighty hand, that he may lift you up in due time. Cast all your anxiety on him because he cares for you."
Association with people who don't know God	Separate yourself from sinners and people who do wrong.	We are to live among the lost. We are not to be separate from them but to live among them in order to reach them. The lost are a primary focus.	1 Corinthians 5:9-11 – "I have written you in my letter not to associate with sexually immoral people—not at all meaning the people of this world who are immoral, or the greedy and swindlers, or idolaters. In that case you would have to leave this world. But now I am writing you that you must not associate with anyone who calls himself a brother but is sexually immoral or greedy, an idolater or a slanderer, a drunkard or a swindler. With such a man do not even eat."
Sharing your faith	Faith and belief in God is a private thing, not to be broadcast with others. Don't offend anyone.	You are to be ready to share your testimony and live your life as an example of God's love.	1 Peter 3:15-16 – "But in your hearts set apart Christ as Lord. Always be prepared to give an answer to everyone who asks you to give the reason for the hope that you have. But do this with gentleness and respect, keeping a clear conscience, so that those who speak maliciously against your good behavior in Christ may be ashamed of their slander."
Work	Get as much as you can with as little work as possible.	Be the best at whatever you do to represent excellence in Christ.	Colossians 3:23-24 – "Whatever you do, work at it with all your heart, as working for the Lord, not for men, since you know that you will receive an inheritance from the Lord as a reward. It is the Lord Christ you are serving."

Page 70:

Q: These folks seem to be trying to defy gravity. Is that the way it is to live according to God's value system/Kingdom thinking? Explain.

The note at the bottom of this page refers to *Conformed to His Image* on page 67 where Ken Boa states:

> "People think they want pleasure, recognition, popularity, status, and power, but the pursuit of these things leads to emptiness, delusion, and foolishness. God has set eternity in our hearts (Ecclesiastes 3:11), and our deepest desires are fulfillment (love, joy, peace), reality (that which does not fade away), and wisdom (skill in living). The only path to this true fulfillment lies in consciously choosing God's value system over what this world offers."

Page 72:

II. The Church and How Do I Relate?

Q: We have Christ, the Holy Spirit and the Bible, so can't we go it alone and be a good Christian without the involvement of others?

A: Not according to Scripture. In 1 Corinthians 12:14, it says, "For in fact the body is not one member but many" and in the following verses God indicates that all members are significant. Additionally, read Hebrews 10:24, 25 together and discuss what may keep people from attending church on a regular basis.

Page 73:

Q: As we read in 1 Corinthians 12:15, aren't some parts of the Body more important than others? Explain.

The "One Anothers"

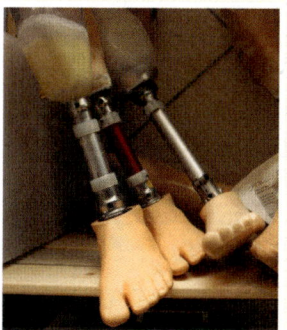

Romans 15:7	Accept one another
Galatians 5:13	Serve one another
Galatians 6:2	Carry one another's burdens
Ephesians 4:2	Bear with one another in love

Additional "One Anothers" not in *Life Perspectives*:

Ephesians 5:21	Submit to one another out of reverence to Christ
Philippians 2:3,4	Consider others better than yourself
Colossians 3:16	Teach and admonish one another with all wisdom
1 Thessalonians 4:18	Encourage one another
1 John 4:7	Love one another

Encourage Timothy to apply the above Scriptures at home as well as at church. Discuss the implications of serving your spouse, accepting him/her unconditionally, etc. Also, note that growth in our spiritual lives does not happen in a vacuum. We see in the above verses Christians relating to one another. We are told to accept one another, to serve one another, to bear one another's burdens in love, to share with those in need, to forgive each other, to look not only after one's own interests but also the interests of others, and more.

Q: What would your church be like if the people who attend would practice these principles as stated above?

Page 74:

Q: Are you thriving in your church? How about your spouse? Your children? How could it be better from your perspective?

Spend some time discussing the "Absolute Basics in Any Assembly or Church" at the bottom of page 74.

Be gentle and go slowly. Don't encourage Timothy to leave a church without considering the possible reactions of Timothy's spouse, children and other family members. The goal of this study is to allow Timothy to discover what God has revealed about the church and to pray that God will guide Timothy as the Scriptures become more and more real.

Page 75:

III. Prosperity and Success

★ Emphasize this question from the book.

Q: How would you define prosperity? Success?

As Timothy is becoming more mature in Christ, you may want to ask him how his view of prosperity or success has changed over the last year.

Page 76:

Q: How can money be a trap? How much does money control your behavior and emotions?

For additional insight into God's view of success, read Joshua 1:8. Notice two requirements for prosperity: (1) "meditate" on the Scriptures (2) do everything they command. Be sure Timothy understands that following these directives do not always mean financial prosperity – God chooses to whom he will give material wealth and to whom he will not.

Page 78:

★ Emphasize this question from the book.

Q: For you personally, what would be a reasonable picture of contentment?

Page 79:

IV. Stewardship

★ Emphasize this question from the book.

Q: What difference would this perspective ('that God owns everything') make in how you view life and resources?

Page 82:

There is nothing we handle that reveals our hearts like the way we handle money.

Q: Are you a wise steward? Explain.

A suggestion for Timothy:

As you discuss this very important principle of Stewardship and giving, it would be a good time to suggest that giving to the CBMC Ministry is a practical opportunity to apply what he has learned from this chapter.

Memory Verse: Kingdom Perspectives

Q: How does this Scripture Memory Verse capture the key point of this lesson?

Next Steps

1. Set a day and time to get together again.
2. Encourage your Timothy to consider the Additional Resources, the Optional Applications, and listen to the audio for this chapter on CD or at operationtimothy.com.
3. Assign Chapter 6, "Your Calling as an Insider."
4. Make a note of any questions you could not answer using the Notes section at the end of each chapter.
5. Update your diary and pray for your Timothy this week.

Notes

Chapter 6: Your Calling as an Insider

The Big Idea: To ensure that Timothy understands God brings us into a relationship with Him, not just for our benefit, but that we might bring others to Him as a result. Our family, friends, neighbors and work relationships are the unique and primary mission field in which God has placed us and to which God has called us.

Key Teaching Points

- An "insider" is "in the world" and therefore can relate to searching people in his areas of personal influence without being perceived as too preachy, while at the same time not embracing values and behaviors that are "of the world."

- To be effective, an insider must have common ground with non-believers.

- We are more effective if we work as a team with other believers.

- Busyness and over-commitment will render us ineffective as an insider.

Teaching Outline

I. What is an Insider?
    To be an effective influence on our culture we must live "in" society without becoming influenced by society – it is the principle of "common ground."

II. How can I be an Insider?
    God has us positioned right where He wants us. Our role is to prepare for the battle, not run from it.

III. How can I survive as an Insider?
    Christ living within us combined with the fellowship of the Christian community will sustain us. Our use of time and resources give us margin for ministry.

IV. What is an Insider's vision?
    To be effective, an insider must envision his or her role as an integral part of a great army whose mission is to help fulfill the Great Commission. Our significance is not determined by wisdom, power or wealth, but by our relationship with God. Understanding God's perspective on work and provision is essential to carrying out this vision.

As you prepare for your time with Timothy, read Chapter 2 of Jim Petersen's *Lifestyle Discipleship*. Petersen's insights regarding the concept of "insiders" will prove helpful. He also has a book dedicated to this topic, *The Insider: Bringing the Kingdom of God into Your Everyday World*. Another book that deals with the reality of the time crunch and over-commitment is Dr. Richard Swensen's classic, *Margin: Restoring Emotional, Physical, Financial, and Time Reserves to Overloaded Lives*.

Page 85:

Begin by reviewing I Chronicles 29:11-12 as well as previously assigned memory verses.

That's What They Say

chapter 6 - your calling as an insider

Read aloud the quotes from Jim Petersen and Charles Swindoll regarding serving as insiders in an unbelieving world.

Q: Why do you think serving on the inside is difficult for most people? What factors tend to pull us away?

Page 86:

I. What is an Insider?

Read this definition to Timothy. The term insider means one who lives in the world, but is not of the world. He recognizes that where he lives and works is God's unique and primary mission field for him.

Page 88:

Q: Does this concept of being an Insider challenge any beliefs or teachings that you have embraced in the past? How so?

Many of Timothy's questions will be answered as you move through the study. This would be a good time to encourage Timothy to begin thinking about being a part of a *Living Proof* small group study.

Looking for Areas of Common Ground

This list is meant to challenge our comfort zones. There may be some areas we need to rethink and others that are obviously not appropriate. However, Timothy may be still young enough in the faith as to be unaware of potential stumbling blocks in some of these areas. Work through the list and discussion various concerns.

Page 89:

Q: Paul describes his insidership in 1 Corinthians 9:19-23. What would it be like if we really personalized this message? How would our lives change?

II. How Can I be an Insider?

Read 1 Peter 2:12 aloud. Note that the preceding verse says we are to abstain from sinful desires while the remainder of the passage speaks to what we should do. Here is the balance of being in and not being of the world. If Timothy is using this insider concept as an excuse to indulge sinful habits, discuss these verses and the implications.

Page 92:

III. How Can I Survive as an Insider?

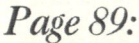 Emphasize these questions from the book.

Q: How can we leverage our activities and relationships for the cause of Christ?

Q: Who are you holding onto as you walk through life versus who is holding onto you?

BK3: 24

Page 94:

IV. What is an Insider's Vision?

Q: How would your actions and attitudes differ towards individuals if you are praying for them? (Reminder: use Ten Most Wanted card)

Meditating on John 15

The entire fifteenth chapter of John can be used as an exercise in meditation, especially for the power source of all of Christian living and specifically for the issue of insiders and margin. Spend some time meditating on the analogy of the vine and the branches. If you have time, read through the chapter and discuss your insights.

Page 95:

Smooth Sailing

Q: Do you ever "step back" from the hectic activity of everyday life and consider where you are heading? What is your vision for the future?

Read the following quote by Charles Swindoll from *Killing Giants, Pulling Thorns*: "**Busyness rapes relationships.** It substitutes shallow frenzy for deep friendship. It promises satisfying dreams, but delivers hollow nightmares. It feeds the ego, but starves the inner man. It fills the calendar but fractures the family. It cultivates a program, but plows under priorities."

Take an Insider Inventory

Work through the list of people Timothy has included on the chart, "I Am an Insider." Focus on the kind of time being spent with each: quality and quantity. Determine if there are some areas that are out of balance; if so, point out the possibilities to Timothy. Discuss opportunities and possible hurdles for building close relationships.

Q: How are you doing in giving these people quality time and quantity time? Are there people listed (or not listed) with whom you want to develop a closer relationship? What are the hurdles? What would you have to change in order to have the time? Do you have relationships with lost people?

Page 96:

Marginal Success

Carefully ask questions about the various areas of Timothy's life and adjust the gauges if necessary. Make a point to share any struggles that you are having and how you are trying to adjust your time commitments to resolve them.

Calling and Work

Note: Calling – in Webster's 1828 Dictionary, we see that a calling can be "a vocation, profession, trade, usual occupation or employment" or a "Divine summons, vocation or invitation."

Page 98:

Q: Is one's calling and work the same? What about for us as Christians?

Page 99:

★ Emphasize these questions from the book.

Q: Read 2 Corinthians 5:18-19. What do these verses indicate is our job description (regardless of vocation)?

Q: Can we fulfill our calling even in work that is not considered high-profile, glamorous or exciting? Describe?

Read aloud and discuss the quote by Ken Boa on page 100.

Memory Verse: Your Calling as an Insider

Q: How does this Scripture Memory Verse capture the key point of this lesson?

Next Steps

1. Set a day and time to get together again.

2. Encourage your Timothy to consider the Additional Resources, the Optional Applications, and listen to the audio for this chapter on CD or at operationtimothy.com.

3. Assign Chapter 7, "Multiplying Your Life."

4. Make a note of any questions you could not answer using the Notes section at the end of each chapter.

5. Update your diary and pray for your Timothy this week.

Chapter 7: Multiplying Your Life

The Big Idea: To give Timothy a vision for spiritual reproduction.

Key Teaching Points

- Discipling is like parenting. It requires sacrifice, perseverance, and dependence on the Holy Spirit.
- Discipling is a transformation process in the context of a relationship. It works from the inside out.
- The goal of discipleship is being Christ-like.
- We are to be intentional about discipling others.
- God calls us to live a life of fruitfulness – spiritual multiplication and reproduction.

Teaching Outline

I. Discipleship: Spiritual Parenting

　i. True discipleship is not knowledge and/or religious activity; it is about a relationship with Christ. The disciplemaker considers the disciple his child until he is mature in Christ.

　ii. Christ provided requirements for His disciples.

II. The Process of Growth
Authentic Christian growth or transformation comes from the inside out. It starts with worldview, changing values and resulting behavior. A biblical worldview is formed based on Scripture.

III. The Goal in Discipleship: Christ is Formed in You

　i. Principles of Discipleship: Relational, Process, Spiritual and Deductive

　ii. Timothy is not dependent on you, but on Christ's life in him.

IV. Life on Life
Discipleship is not a curriculum, but an opportunity for Timothy to observe, ask questions, think through choices and weigh events through the teachings of Scripture with you.

V. Finding a Timothy
We can't disciple everyone, so we must select men who are faithful, available, and teachable. For Timothy to begin discipling a person, he should pray. An individual goes through spiritual stages in becoming a Christian, from unbeliever to discipler.

VI. Spiritual Reproduction: Multiplication
God's plan is low-key. He wants each one of His children to transfer what he knows and has to another one of His children, who will in turn transfer what he knows to another.

As you prepare for your time with Timothy, read Chapter 4 of Jim Petersen's *Lifestyle Discipleship*.

Page 103:

Begin by reviewing 1 Corinthians 7:24 as well as previously assigned memory verses.

Q: What do you see in this picture? How is it a metaphor for life?

I. Discipleship: Spiritual Parenting

Page 105:

Spiritual Parenting

Q: What was it like when you helped your child or a young person accomplish some skill or achieve a goal?

Spend some time on this chart, describing how evangelism is like farming and discipleship is like parenting. Talk about the needs of a baby or child and how their needs are protection and love. And as the child matures, his needs change and the father figure is to encourage and to equip. In the maturation process, the disciple becomes an adult and understands the purpose for his life – "to join Him in developing His Kingdom on this earth and in the hearts and minds of individual men and women." (This last sentence is from page 103, *That's What they Say*.)

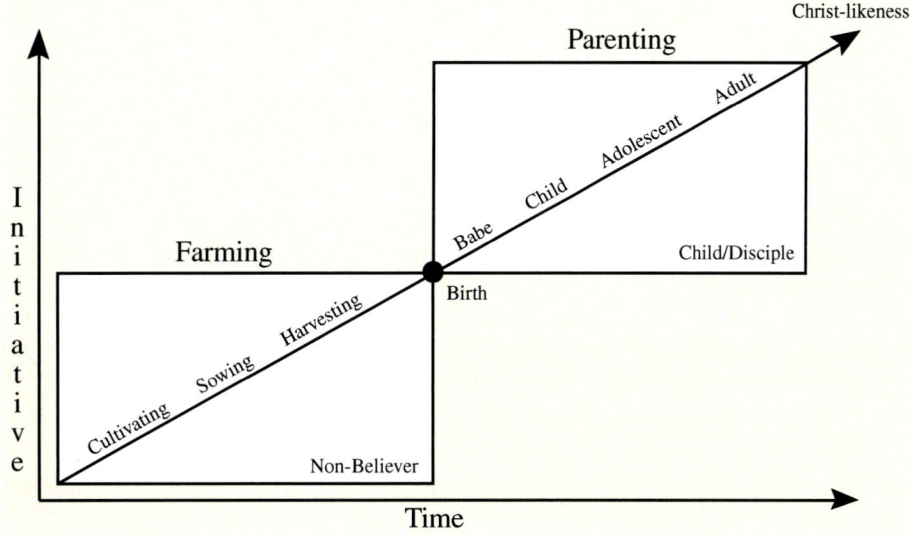

In Chuck Swindoll's book, *Growing up in God's Family*, he describes the process of growing up in the following chart:

The Ages and Stages of Growing Up			
	Description	Statement	Focus
Birth/Infancy	Immaturity	"Help me!"	Surviving
Childhood	Discovery	"Tell me!"	Learning
Adolescence	Irresponsibility	"Show me!"	Challenging
Adulthood	Maturity	"Follow me!"	Serving

Page 108:

Q: Why do you think helping others to become disciples is difficult, messy, and long-term?

Don't be discouraged. By example, keep your focus on Jesus, not a task, an organization, or self-fulfillment. Remember, Hebrews 12:1,2 "… let us throw off everything that hinders and the sin that so easily entangles, and let us run with perseverance the race marked out for us. Let us fix our eyes on Jesus, the author and perfecter of our faith…"

Page 109:

II. The Process of Growth

Q: Which has more to do with developing character: worldview or behavior? Why?

To be is to do, or who you are determines what you do.

Q: How would you fill the center of the circle? What are the four or five major values that motivate your life?

"Authentic Christian growth comes from the inside and works its way to the surface."

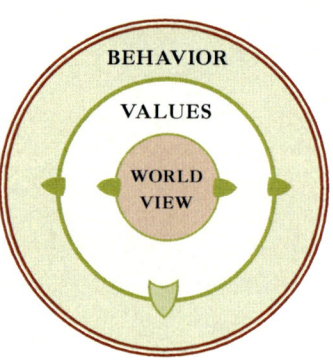

Page 111:

III. The Goal: Christ is Formed in You

Q: Do you see that both the man and the boy are looking in the same direction? How is this analogous to the discipling process?

A: Both must keep their focus on Christ (Hebrews 12:1-2).

Christ Our Life

Definition: Deductive - of or pertaining to deduction; capable of being deduced from premises; deducible.

Page 114:

Q: Did you ever put on your father's shoes when you were a young boy? Why did you want to imitate your father?

IV. Life on Life: Discipleship is a Life to Life Relationship

Operation Timothy is a systematic and logical approach, but we must be sensitive to the needs of the person and the leading of the Holy Spirit.

Page 115:

Q: Why is discipling more than just lessons, information, and techniques?

Depending on the answer Timothy gives, spend some time on the "Discovery Process" and the principles outlined by Walt Henrichsen on page 117.

Page 119:

V. Finding a Timothy

Q: Why is it important to be intentional about looking for a Timothy?

Q: Why do you think Jesus told us to "go and make disciples"?

[Hint: Who matures through discipleship?]

Page 120:

The Spiritual Awareness Chart (see next page) is helpful in evaluating where a person might be in his spiritual journey.

Page 121:

VI. Spiritual Reproduction: A Final Challenge

Q: How are dominos falling more like spiritual reproduction than a college graduation?

Memory Verse: Multiplying Your Life

Q: How does this Scripture Memory Verse capture the key point of this lesson?

Next Steps

1. Review Matthew 28:19, 20.

2. Set another time to review all the verses in *Operation Timothy*.

3. Encourage Timothy to make a commitment to another study, either with you or with a small group.

Spiritual Awareness Chart

Sanctification	**Stage IV** **Discipling** Maturing Process Disciple = Reproduced life of Christ Emphasis: Life-on-life relationships	+4 +3 +2 +1	Going! Mobilized to reproduce Maturing into Christ-likeness Settling into a caring community Grounding in faith
Regeneration			**New Creature**
	Stage III **Harvesting** Picking the Crop The Grain = A Decision for Jesus Christ Emphasis: Encourage a meaningful decision of faith	-1 -2 -3 -4 -5	Repenting and believing Deciding to act Recognizing personal need Positive attitude toward Gospel Grasping implications of Gospel
Conviction	**Stage II** **Sowing** Planting the Seed The Seed = Gospel Truth Emphasis: Presenting the Gospel, understanding the truth.	-6 -7 -8 -9	Aware of Gospel basics Positive attitude toward the Bible Aware of Bible's relevance Aware of difference in messenger
General Revelation	**Stage I** **Cultivation** Preparing the Soil The Soil = Human Hearts Emphasis: Building a friendship bridge	-10 -11 -12	Positive attitude toward messenger Aware of messenger Going his own way
God's Role	**Our Role**		**Mini-Decisions** Some of the specific decisions that could be made.

(Rejection spans from -6 to -12)

Conclusions and Recommendations

Congratulate Timothy on completing this part of his journey in getting to know God more intimately. Reinforce the fact that this is only the beginning. The following are a few suggestions on the next steps you might take to help Timothy continue growing toward Christ-likeness:

1. Study the *Operation Timothy Leader's Guide* together. It's available in print or Timothy can go to operationtimothy.com and register as a Paul to gain access to the leader's guide PDFs.

2. Help Timothy find his own Timothy:
   He should look for people who have the following characteristics:

   a. Heart for God

   b. Teach-ability

   c. Faithfulness

   d. Willingness to teach others

   Have Timothy make a list of people who have these qualities or the potential to develop them and pray for them. His Timothy may be a person he had the privilege of leading to Christ. He may be an immature Christian or a non-Christian who is willing to explore God's Word, perhaps someone on his Ten Most Wanted card.

3. CBMC has produced two dramatic video series called *Living Proof* that illustrates the process of evangelism and discipleship. You may want to consider these studies as a next step for your Timothy as you wrap up *Operation Timothy*.

4. Encourage him to continue to dig deep into God's Word. One idea is to do an Advanced ABC Bible study on the book of 1 Thessalonians (see page 12 of *Life Perspectives*). Also, have Timothy continue to memorize and meditate on Scripture. He may like to use the Navigators' Topical Memory System.

5. Encourage Timothy to read Jim Petersen's books, *Living Proof* and *Lifestyle Discipleship* and Dr. Richard Swenson's book, *Margin*.

6. Encourage Timothy to begin attending CBMC Family Conferences with his family. Other Christian conferences and seminars may greatly enhance his growth in the Lord also.

7. Help Timothy develop a Life Purpose Statement. See the following pages for guidance on this one.

Assembling a Life Purpose Statement

Life ad lib. In the middle of a battle in *Raiders of the Lost Ark*, Indiana Jones is asked about his plan. "I don't know," he answers, "I'm kind of making it up as I go along." For most people, life is like that: an unpredictable adventure with no set destination or course to get there. From our activities, we conclude what our purpose has been. A wise planner begins with purpose, and moves to activities.

What does Jesus' parable in Matthew 7:24-27 say about the foundation for living?

___

___

Steps to building a Purpose Statement

First you'll need to do some heavy thinking, praying, and writing. Use these questions as a worksheet.

1. Start from our common purpose as Christians.

Based on our earlier study, what does God desire from us all? Nothing in the rest of your statement can be inconsistent with Gods commands, and you won't be successful in other goals if you ignore His purposes.

2. Who are you?

What is your marital status? Family plan? Occupational status? What special skills are you equipped with? These must all be taken into account.

3. What are your dreams?

God gives us special vision and aspiration about things we desire to happen. When they are in accordance with His laws, they can be a clue to His will for us.

4. What are your spiritual gifts, skills, temperament, etc?

5. What impressions are you gaining through prayer? Don't plan without praying.

6. What do godly friends say? Their perspective is essential.

7. Now take the common purpose and integrate with the other questions to begin to write a purpose statement. (Create a rough draft.)

Name

God's universal purpose

Your unique gifts, skills, temperament, etc.

Career goals

Family goals

Personal goals

What Scripture verses has God used in your life to give you direction and purpose? Choose one that best characterizes God's purpose for your life.

_____

_____

_____

_____

_____

Be patient: this may take several times of rewriting over a period of time to refine and polish. Discuss this with some close personal friends. Talk to someone who has done this. Ask them to share their purpose statement with you and share how they arrived at it. Sign your name at the bottom of your statement. (If married, this should be done together.)

"A longing fulfilled is sweet to the soul..." Proverbs 13:19

Following are samples of purpose statements from two different couples to give you some idea of how yours might look. Try to write your own in light of the specific gifts and unique calling God has entrusted to you. Remember, these were developed over a period of time, re-evaluated periodically, refined, updated. So, just start simply.

If you need more in-depth guidance, *Establishing Your Purpose* gives detailed instructions and help in preparing a life purpose statement. You may buy this via the CBMC store at www.cbmc.com/store.

LIFE PURPOSE STATEMENT
(SAMPLE #1)

Life Purpose Verses

1 Thessalonians 2:8–"So being affectionately desirous of you, we were willing to have imparted unto you, not the gospel of God only, but also our own souls, because you were dear unto us."

2 Corinthians 12:15–"And I will very gladly spend and be spent for you; though the more abundantly I love you the less I be loved."

1. To devote my life, to and with my wife (as one), to see that every immediate member of our family becomes a godly Christian. This includes our sons-in-law, their wives (our daughters), grandchildren and grandchildren's children. We will spend time with them as a group and individually in the activities that promote godliness, spending our energy and resources as needed for the accomplishment of this.

2. Our home is given to us by God and shall always be available to Him for everything He wishes to use it for.

3. All our earthly resources belong to God and are available to Him. We are stewards (managers) to utilize these resources as we are directed by God. We will give the tithe regularly as a minimum. The major purpose of the accumulation of our money and resources is to continue our goals after we have gone to Heaven.

4. As much as is possible, we will direct our everyday work and play activities toward the CBMC purpose which we have been called to, and which we feel is synonymous with the Great Commission (Matthew 28: 19-20).

5. We will seize every opportunity presented to us to share Jesus Christ as the only Savior and Lord and answer for the sin of individual man. We depend upon the Holy Spirit for our direction in these matters as we understand that this battle for people's souls is supernatural.

6. We are committed to the training of a few people personally as disciplemakers and leaders. Understanding that this takes a tremendous amount of energy and time, we plan 2-8 years with individual people that God entrusts to us.

7. We remain open to the Lord for every new learning experience. We desire to grow spiritually and realize that God keeps us in a training program. It is our desire to be in this learning program until we are promoted to Heaven and our eternal promises.

8. We are learning to establish goals for each category stated and want the Lord to hold us accountable for setting and maintaining this LIFE PURPOSE statement. Each of these statements should be broken into segments reflecting both short-range and long-range goals. These should be checked monthly, noted for progress quarterly and updated for accuracy and accomplishment yearly. We will schedule regular time on a calendar for planning and prayer.

LIFE PURPOSE STATEMENT
(SAMPLE #2)

My Purpose:

"Love the Lord my God with all my heart and with all my soul and with all my mind… Love my neighbor as myself" (Matthew 22:37-38).

1. Love the Lord my God with all my heart, all my soul, and all my mind.

    a. Make time daily getting to know and love God more intimately, through reading the Bible, prayer, memorizing, meditating and applying Scripture to every area of my life (spiritual, emotional, physical, spouse, children, work, leisure, friends, family, etc.)

    b. Spend time daily with my wife and children getting to know God through family devotions, attending family conferences, Bible studies. Take each child through *Operation Timothy* when he/she is old enough and spiritually ready to receive it.

    c. Worship and study with other believers at least weekly.

    d. Ongoing, personal Bible study that deepens my understanding of and love for God in Scripture.

2. Love my neighbor as myself.

    a. Take care of myself as a cherished, valuable creation of God Himself. This includes balance of physical exercise and nutrition, spiritual growth, emotional outlets of play, meaningful friendships and relationships, rest, work. I know that I depend upon God to fill up my tank in these areas so that I might give to others from a full, not empty, tank.

    b. Love the "neighbors" God has put in my life: my spouse first, my children, my extended family, friends, neighbors, co-workers, and others. This includes spending quality and quantity time with each of them in getting to know each other, playing together, sharing Christ, meeting each other's needs, worshipping together.

    c. Ask God to give me one person, of the same sex, that I can spiritually parent through *Operation Timothy*. Meet with him/her regularly in Bible study, and frequently for fun activities.

    d. Give to my local church, missionaries, and Christian organizations as the Lord leads me.

GOALS TO FACILITATE A LIFE PURPOSE STATEMENT

EXAMPLES

	Goals	Purpose	Verse
FAMILY	1. Read God's Word together daily and memorize Scripture.	To strengthen family bonds and put God's words in our heart.	Deuteronomy 6:6-7
	2. Spend time with spouse and children daily — education and sports.	To educate our children in the ways of the Lord.	
	3. Eliminate television.		
SPIRITUAL	1. To read through Bible in a year, using Daily Walk Bible.	To know God better, to understand His will for our lives, and to have a more abundant life.	John 17:3
	2. Increase our prayer time — maintain a prayer journal.		
FINANCIAL	1. To live within our budget.	To keep from increasing our debt and to begin laying aside the financial weights that hinder our life purpose.	Proverbs 22:7
	2. To get out of debt.		
PHYSICAL	1. Ride the bike every weekday early in the morning.	To maintain our health, lean bodies, and to be joyful and appealing witnesses.	Hebrews 12:11
SOCIAL	1. To stay active with Christian and non-Christian couples and friends.	To be effective salt and light, to reach others for Christ.	Matthew 5:13
	2. To be on-time all of the time.		

INDEX OF OPERATION TIMOTHY BOOKS

Optional Application Suggestions

Movies:

Amazing Grace (2006)
The *Jesus* Film (1979)
Luther (2003)
Indiana Jones series
The Lion, The Witch, and The Wardrobe (2005)
The Mission (1986)
It's a Wonderful Life (1946)
Chariots of Fire (1981)

Music:

"A Celebration," by U2
"In God We Trust" by Rachel Lampa
"Give Me Jesus" by Fernando Ortega
"Change the World (Lost Ones)," by Anberlin
"All I Need Is Everything," by Over the Rhine

Recommended Resources

www.everystudent.com
www.jcstudies.com
www.storyspot.com

Absolute Surrender, Andrew Murray
Amazing Grace, by Eric Metaxas
The Case for Christ, Lee Strobel
Choose the Life: Exploring a Faith that Embraces Discipleship, Bill Hull
Classic Christianity, Bob George
Conformed to His Image, Ken Boa
Disappointment with God, Philip Yancey
Establishing Your Purpose, Vision Foundation
Everyman's Battle, Stephen Arterburn and Fred Stoeker
Evidence that Demands a Verdict, Josh McDowell
Experiencing God, Henry Blackaby
Five Love Languages, Dr. Gary Chapman
The Fruit of the Spirit, John Sanderson
Halftime, Bob Buford
Heaven, Randy Alcorn
"How Can the Bible be Authoritative?" by N.T. Wright
How Good is Good Enough? by Andy Stanley
How to Read the Bible for All It's Worth, Gordon Fee and Douglas Stuart
How to Study the Bible, John MacArthur
How to Study Your Bible, Kay Arthur
Incomparable Christ, The Person and Work of Jesus Christ, J. Oswald Chambers
Is Jesus the Only Savior?, by James R. Edwards
The Jesus I Never Knew, by Phillip Yancey
A Journey to Victorious Praying, Bill Thrasher
Knowing God, J.I. Packer
Language of Love, Dr. Gary Smalley
Letters to Malcolm: Chiefly on Prayer, C.S. Lewis
Lifestyle Evangelism, Joe Aldrich
Lifestyle Discipleship, Jim Petersen
Living by the Book: The Art and Science of Reading the Bible, Howard & William Hendricks
Living Free in Christ, Neil Anderson
Living Proof DVDs, CBMC
Living Proof, Jim Petersen
Locking Arms, Stu Weber
Louder Than Words, Andy Stanley
Love & Respect, Dr. Emerson Eggerichs
Man in the Mirror, Pat Morley
Mere Christianity, C. S. Lewis
More Than a Carpenter, by Josh McDowell
"One Second After You Die," by Mark Cahill
Prayer: A Holy Occupation, Oswald Chambers
The Pursuit of God, A. W. Tozer
The Screwtape Letters, C.S. Lewis
The Strategy of Satan, Warren Wiersbe
Release of the Spirit, Watchman Nee
The Truth Project, Focus of the Family
True Spirituality, Francis A. Schaeffer
Victory Over the Darkness, Neil Anderson
What's So Amazing About Grace, by Philip Yancey
When People Are Big and God Is Small, Edward Welch
Your Money Counts, Howard Dayton
Multiple resources from Crown Financial Ministries

Most of these resources are not provided by CBMC, but can be purchased, rented, or borrowed through a variety of outlets. The music, suggested as a way to find common ground with your Timothy, can probably be found online.

Topical Index (book: page number)

ABC Bible Study	3: 12-13
accountability	3: 49
Adams, John	3: 1
Adsit, Chris	3: 112
Alcorn, Randy	3: 77
Anderson, Sherwood	3: 53
Allen, Woody	1: 25
ancient manuscripts	1: 17
anxiety	2: 89
Assisi, Francis	2: 99
Augustine	2: 81
Aurelius, Marcus	1: 1
autism	2: 81
Barber, Wayne	2: 62
Barnhouse, Donald Grey	2: 1, 99
Barth, Karl	1: 51
Beechner, John	2: 18
Bible	1: 13-22; 2: 3, 12, 56; 3: 1-14, 74, 81
Blackaby, Henry	3: 17
Blackaby, Richard	2: 81
Boa, Ken	1: 32; 2: 21, 25, 66, 74; 3: 64, 70, 81, 100
bondage	2: 25-26, 38
Bonhoeffer, Dietrich	3: 58
ten Boom, Corrie	2: 81
Bruce, F.F.	1: 43
Buñuel, Luis	1: 25
Carter-Scott, Cherie	1: 63
Chapman, Gary	3: 62
Chesterton, G.K.	3: 53
Christ Jesus	1: 39-48, 52-60; 2: 18, 26, 42, 46, 72; 3: 5, 17, 89, 114
church	3: 71-74
common ground	3: 89
community	3: 41, 53-54, 57-58, 74, 92, 104, 117
contentment	3: 77-78
Cowper, William	2: 33
Crabb, Larry	3: 54
critical process	3: 105
crucifixion	1: 57
The Da Vinci Code	1: 13
devil, Satan	2: 23, 29, 33, 41-44
Diana, princess	3: 85
discipleship	3: 104-123
displacement	2: 60
Dobson, James	1: 10
Dryden, John	2: 49
Dungy, Tony	3: 40
Dylan, Bob	3: 17
Edwards, Jonathan	3: 123
Eifert, Lorenz	1: 51
Eims, Leroy	3: 103
Einstein, Albert	1: 1, 39
Elliott, Jim	3: 67
Epictetus	2: 17
Epp, Theodore	3: 86
eternal life	2: 6, 8, 12
faith	1: 27, 41; 2: 1, 115; 3: 25, 69
F.A.T.	3: 118
Ferguson, David	3: 63
Fields, W.C.	1: 13
Fisher, Mel	2: 1
Fitzsimmons, Cotton	2: 18
five love languages	3: 62
flesh	2: 40
forgiveness	1: 63-72; 2: 54
Fowler, James	2: 1

Franklin, Benjamin	3: 67	Lewis, C.S.	1: 25, 51; 2: 1, 29, 33, 49, 99; 3: 68
freedom	2: 26	Lincoln, Abraham	2: 82
gambling	2: 61	Little, Paul	3: 24
Gandhi, Mahatma	1: 52	love	2: 24, 26, 59; 3: 62, 117
Gillham, Bill	2: 21, 23	Luce, Ron	2: 34
God the Father	1: 26, 34-36; 2: 7, 17, 19, 38, 81, 88; 3:3	Luther, Martin	2: 81
Gordon, Ernest	1: 64	margin	3: 95-96
Graham, Billy & Ruth	1: 15-16; 2: 81	marriage	3: 59-64
Gregory of Nazianzus	1: 54	McCandless, Chris	2: 49
grip on God's Word	3: 10	McGill, Bryant H.	1: 63
Havel, Václav	1: 2	McGrath, Alister	2: 65
Hendricks, Howard	2: 2; 3: 103, 118	meditation	3: 10
Henrichsen, Walt	2: 49; 3: 33, 117, 122	memorize Scripture	2: 12-13
Hitchens, Christopher	1: 25	Merton, Thomas	2: 33
Hoffer, Eric	3: 53	miracles	1: 54-55
Mr. Holland's Opus	1: 7	money	1: 3, 32; 3: 76-77, 79, 81-82
Holy Spirit	2: 28-29, 65-78, 114; 3: 20, 25, 41	Moody, Dwight	2: 17; 3: 33
Hovey, E. Paul	3: 1	Morley, Patrick	1: 29; 3: 49-50
Houssaye, Arsène	2: 17	Mueller, George	3: 25-26
Hull, Bill	3: 106	Napoleon	1: 39
Ibsen, Henrik	1: 51	Nietzshe, Friedrich	1: 1
identity	2: 17-26; 3: 33, 97, 113-114	Niles, D. T.	2: 99
		Nouwen, Henri	3: 57
insider	3: 85-100	one anothers	3: 55, 73
inspired, "God-breathed"	1: 21; 2: 56	Packer, J. I.	2: 65, 100; 3: 20
It's a Wonderful Life	1: 6	Parker, T.H.L.	3: 1
Joan of Arc	2: 17	peace	1: 72; 2: 39, 90; 3: 78
Jackson, Gordon	3: 18	perfection	1: 67
Jefferson, Thomas	1: 39	Petersen, Jim	3: 41, 58, 67, 74, 85-86, 106, 110, 112, 114
Keller, Helen	3: 33		
Kierkegaard, Soren	1: 1, 6	Phillips, J. B.	1: 25
Kingdom of God	3: 68-70	Pinnock, Clark	1: 60
Latourette, Kenneth	1: 40	Piper, John	2: 50
Lee, Robert E.	3: 2	Pippert, Rebecca Manley	2: 99

Operation Timothy Index

prayer	2: 81-96; 3: 26, 118-119
prayer, unanswered	2: 86
prophecy	1: 20
purpose	1: 5-7; 3: 46, 103
quiet time	2: 94
Ravenhill, Leonard	3: 17
redemption	1: 70
relationships	1: 31-32; 2: 26; 3: 53-64
repentance	2: 9
resurrection	1: 58-60
River Kwai	1: 64
Robin Hood	2: 44
Roman Empire	1: 59
Roosevelt, Theodore	3: 34
Ross, Hugh	1: 19
Ruskin, John	2: 33
salvation	2: 9-10, 28
Schaff, Philip	1: 49
Seven Elements of Spiritual Transformation	3: 41
Shakespeare	1: 1; 2: 49
Shaw, George Bernard	1: 13
significance	1: 3, 5; 2: 19-20, 25-26
Silvoso, Ed	2: 33
sin	1: 45, 51, 67, 71; 2: 51, 54, 102-103
Smedes, Lewis	1: 63-64
smoking	2: 2
spiritual armor	2: 37
spiritual awareness chart	3: 120
spiritual gifts	2: 75
spiritual parenting	3: 104-107
Spurgeon, Charles	3: 33
stewardship	3: 78-82
success	1: 3; 2: 17, 28; 3: 75-77
Swindoll, Charles	2: 101; 3: 67, 85, 103
Tarbela Dam	2: 67
temptation	2: 49, 51, 60-61
Ten Most Wanted card	2: 92
testimony	2: 101-105, 113
testimony, tips	2: 110
time	3: 47, 49
timothy, finding a	3: 118-119
Tomlin, Lily	1: 3, 29
top ten marriage needs	3: 63
Trinity	2: 67
Twain, Mark	1: 8, 14; 2: 49; 3: 48
Vanauken, Sheldon	3: 85
Wall Street	1: 3
war	2: 33-35, 37
Weber, Stu	3: 54
Wells, H. G.	1: 39
Westcott, Brooke Foss	1: 58
Wilde, Oscar	2: 49
witnessing	2: 101, 111, 114
worldview	3: 109-110
work	1: 30; 3: 69, 97
Wood, Bryant	1: 19
Yancey, Philip	3: 53

Made in the USA
Coppell, TX
17 February 2020